Translation Spectrum

With Essays by

BEN BENNANI
ALDO S. BERNARDO
HASKELL M. BLOCK
MARCIA NITA DORON
JOSEPH F. GRAHAM
MICHAEL JASENAS
ANDRÉ LEFEVERE
ZOJA PAVLOVSKIS
ANNE E. RODDA
MARILYN GADDIS ROSE
STEPHEN DAVID ROSS
WILLIAM H. SNYDER
SANDRO STICCA
H. STEPHEN STRAIGHT
IMMANUEL WALLERSTEIN
GEORGE E. WELLWARTH

Translation Spectrum

ESSAYS IN THEORY AND PRACTICE

EDITED BY

Marilyn Gaddis Rose

State University of New York Press

ALBANY

A grant from the University Awards Program of the State University of New York and the Research Foundation of the State University of New York assisted in paying the costs of publishing this book.

Published by
State University of New York Press, Albany

© 1981 State University of New York

For information, address State University of New York Press, State University Plaza, Albany, N.Y., 12246

Library of Congress Cataloging in Publication Data

Main entry under title:

Translation Spectrum.

    Bibliography: p.
    Includes index.
    1. Translating and interpreting—Addresses, essays, lectures. I. Rose, Marilyn Gaddis.
P306.T743   418′.02   80-20302

10 9 8 7 6 5 4

Contents

Contents

Translation Spectrum

Introduction: Time and Space
In the Translation Process

by Marilyn Gaddis Rose

Translation is primarily a time-bound process and, when it is of literature, a time art[1]; yet the space it requires cannot be discounted.

It is true, first of all, that we can translate only *after* the fact of the source text. Second, we can translate only sequentially.[2] Third, the timing of a translation is pervasive; i.e., the time of the source text and the time of the translation pervade every factor the translator must consider in translating and every criterion the critic must use in evaluating.

But whatever the text type,[3] whatever the relationship between the source text and target text,[4] the process of transferring it from one language to another has a spatializing component which should not be slighted. We know that bad translations usually result when a translator is merely translating words and does not understand what he is translating.[5] Put more abstractly, he lacks a coherent *Gestalt* of his text.[6] If that is the case, if he does not understand what he is translating as a whole, he is likely to mistranslate even the mere words.

Translators, more often than not, work intuitively and, for the most part, alone. Their choices, even when made routinely through long experience, are made in terms of what sounds right for the text at hand. If they are sure of their choices, they can probably defend them. Yet the fact remains that before a given translation is entirely completed, another mind or minds must be brought to bear. The process itself optimally requires it.

The process may be discussed as a six-step scheme. It should be emphasized that although the steps are discussed sequentially, having a sequential logic, for some translators various steps could be carried on simultaneously. The steps are: (1) preliminary analysis, (2) exhaustive

1

style and content analysis, (3) acclimation of the text, (4) reformulation of the text, (5) analysis of the translation, and (6) review and comparison.[7]

Step 1: preliminary analysis. In preliminary analysis, material is judged worthy of translation. (The translator may have reached this decision himself on the basis of his own taste and interest, or someone else, e.g., an editor or instructor, may have made this initial judgment for him.) All contributors to this anthology begin with the assumption that an affirmative decision has been made in this regard, but we should not minimize how critical this decision is, especially for texts of considerable volume. The bibliographical check recommended by Michael Jasenas should begin here.

Step 2: exhaustive style and content analysis. In style and content analysis we ask, "What makes this literary text literary? What makes this scholarly text authoritative?" If it is a truly congenial literary text, a translator usually feels that his intuition and taste obviate the first question, for the writer to be translated merely happens to be someone else and happens to be using a different language. To cite two of Haskell Block's examples, Baudelaire saw himself in Poe, Nerval saw himself in Heine. Here, to recall pervasive timing, it might be thought that a near-contemporary might have an advantage. If he does—and canonical translations are not necessarily, nor even usually, those made close to the time of the original—it is an opportunity of short duration. If the text is removed in time, or if it is merely interesting, rather than compelling, or if it is a work that should be translated for cultural reasons (i.e., it makes a certain work available to readers who no longer—or never did—cope with the original), then it may be necessary to itemize and hierarchize the text strategies. This may, quite bluntly, amount to problem-solving. Scholarly texts and their authority extend this latter type of analysis. Whereas it might be merely risky for an American to translate Balzac without knowing the Anglo-American tradition of Realism, it could be disastrous to translate Althusser or Negri without a background in Marx and Engels. Further, as Immanuel Wallerstein and Marcia Doron emphasize, it would be unwise to start out without accepted translations of similar works at hand and without a knowledge of the subfield and its current scholarly momentum.

Step 3: acclimation of the text. During acclimation of the text, the translating goes from internal to external. We have told ourselves roughly what the work means, but there have probably been verbal ellipses in our internal translations. Indeed, although we may well have settled certain expressions or key terms in our text-to-be, we have been thinking in the language of the source text. We now work out our own strategies—perhaps compromises—with the form of its message. We decide what is the irreducible invariable and how or if we can preserve it. Sometimes we decide that textual autonomy and prestige require a calque and/or footnoting; see the essays of Zoja Pavlovskis and Sandro Sticca on translating from classical and medieval languages. At other times, we shall have to settle for a workable equivalent or comparable effect; see the essays of Ben Bennani, George E. Wellwarth, and Anne E. Rodda on the special claims of poetry, drama, and music. In short, this is where the actual process of getting from source text to target text may begin.

Step 4: reformulation of the text. It is during reformulation of the text that what is commonly considered translating takes place. All of our verbalizing must be done in the target language now. (This is optimally our native language.) We do, most often, proceed from sentence to sentence. We must choose between alternatives and produce a text that is sequentially complete.[8] Most translators will modify their earlier analyses at this stage. This is because as long as the material remained itself, the expression of its author or an expression in a foreign language, it stayed within that containment. Even if it was ambiguous, it was ambiguous within the parameters of another language system. When we bring it over to our own language, whether we are simply intermediaries (as might be the case with an international treaty) or interpreters (as might be the case with a lyric poem), we alter its parameters. (This inevitability or these risks and their theoretical implications are taken up in the essays of Joseph Graham and Stephen Ross.) Translators often have the experience of believing they understand a text—and they probably do—while, and as long as, it is in the original language, only to find themselves unsettled, if not actually confused, when they must reformulate it in their own language. Indeed, it is far from rare for the bilingual author who works with his translator to decide that the original is confusing and change it, and writers who translate their own works regularly take more liberties than another translator would.[9]

Step 5: analysis of the translation. In translation anaylsis, the translator continues translating but as his own editor and critic. In short, he revises, rarely fewer than three times and, when possible, with a time lapse between revisions. This is when the translation is measured against the larger context of culture, with the related subcontexts of language and rhetorical tradition, which may have been obscured during the strain of sequential translation. This is also when the translation is measured against audience needs or the intended text function. All essays touch on these measurements, although those of André Lefevere, Marilyn Rose, William H. Snyder, and H. Stephen Straight speak to them specifically. Any place where information has been added, subtracted, or skewed should either be rectified or exonerated at this point.[10]

Step 6: review and comparison. The translator hands the translation over to someone else for review and comparison—editor, instructor, supervisor, collaborator. By now it has become the translator's text, and writers are proverbially too close to their work to see it as a reader would. This someone else, the "third reader" (if the translator functions as the "second reader"),[11] can detect lapses or lacunae. In the time of the process, he reads after the problem-solving of acclimation and reformulation have occurred. In the space of the process, he forms his own *Gestalt* of the text in translation. It is usually considered desirable that he know the original text so that he can judge whether comparable effects are achieved or comparable functions served.[12] He might even be called upon to judge whether comparable effects or functions were desirable. (A university press would have at least one outside reader who could compare the original and the translation.) He could judge whether the appropriate rhetorical expectations of the intended target reader were observed. (A commercial press would tend to emphasize this criterion and modify accordingly.)

As process, this much does happen, and it is good that it does. While ultimate translations are never written, canonical ones are. And many useful and effective ones, whether longlived or ephemeral. We should keep in mind while reading the discussions of Graham and Ross that although theoretically translation is almost inconceivable, practically it happens all the time—and rather well. Indeed, the six-step outline just described might lead to the inference that it should be possible to have a perfect translation, if not an ultimate one, every time.

Why don't we? We don't because the translator—or a machine programmed for translation—is not only a component of the time and space he translates in but is himself compounded of time and space. We have described what a translator must do in the approximate order he must do it in, *once* his action can be categorized. We cannot even begin to describe—until much more work is done on artificial intelligence—what goes on in Step 4 *just before* his first word choice comes to him or *just as* he gropes for a word he knows. The X of his temperament and taste, his psychohistory and environment, in volatile interaction with those of the author of the source text and the still more mysterious interaction with those of the intended audience— these are indisputably *données*, but *données* which are not available. The X's are gaps, lacks, absences. In situations of immediacy where covert translations are called for, such interstices may be neither noticeable nor troublesome. It is the initial drafting of a treaty which requires attention, and we may strive for interlanguage texts that are semantic repetitions. Even in covert translations, the interstices may pose problems in time. In overt translations, they are noticeable from the outset. If the interstices are within the range of tolerability, the translation is used—until the range itself becomes intolerable. No *Gestalt*, even of works that seem transparent like a Jules Verne novel, is completely comprehensive. Even when there is a relative consensus, contours change in time, for words enlarge and diminish their referential fields, and the actions and the concepts they describe change in cultural significance. This means that works get retranslated and that works once not needing or not considered worth translating get translated.

This accounts for the dynamism in translation, the spaces a translation successively occupies, first with the translator, a member of a cultural generation, and subsequently with readers of other generations.

NOTES

1. We shall leave aside exceptional procedures in literature such as calligrams, concrete poetry, and any literary form which is in fact a spatialization attempt.

2. A language with a case system may engage us to work out from key words within a sentence rather than from first word to last word. In German, we tend to look at the clause endings for crucial verbs. Further, it is sometimes suggested to translators of long works,

such as novels or monographs, that they work out their initial struggles with the source text at some point midway where the signs of combat will be less obvious to a reader. None of these procedures is really an exception to the inevitable sequence or seriality which must be followed.

3. See Katharina Reiss, *Texttyp und Uebersetzungsmethode* (Kronberg/TS: Scriptor Verlag, 1976), pp. 16-21. Reiss divides texts into informative, expressive, and operative. Her types are discussed in "Translation Types and Conventions," *infra*.

4. Juliane House, in *A Model for Translation Quality Assessment* (Tuebingen: Verlag Gunter Narr, 1977) distinguishes between overt and covert translations. A reader is aware that he is reading an overt translation, e.g., a Russian novel in English translation. The reader of a covert translation, e.g., a multinational business contract, while aware that translation has taken place, regards the piece as a single text in more than one language. Her distinction is discussed in "Translation Types and Conventions," *infra*.

5. This was the "shortcoming" of the first machine translations.

6. Maria Tymoczko, in "Translating Old Irish." Paper presented at the American Literary Translators Association, Dallas, November 13, 1978, points out that with certain dead languages rudimentary segmented translation is the only means of discovering text meaning. However, with her background, she did proceed, from informed conjectures, with her *Gestalt* becoming particularized as she worked on the sagas. Interviewing a cross section of translators in Amsterdam provides verification from translators of another language orientation. See the work of James S. Holmes, "Translation Theory: A Handful of Theses." (Paper delivered at the International Symposium on Achievements in the Theory of Translation, Moscow and Yerevan, October 23-30, 1978); Holmes et al. *Literature and Translation: New Perspectives in Literary Studies* (Louvain: Acco, 1978), pp. 29-82.

7. These have a partial correlation with George Steiner's hermeneutic motion exposed in chapter five of *After Babel* (New York: Oxford Press, 1975), pp. 296-513. Preliminary analysis corresponds to his trust, an act of faith that there is something to be translated. Exhaustive style and content analysis corresponds to his penetration, aggression, and comprehension. Acclimation and reformulation together comprise his embodiment. Analysis of the translation and review and comparison should ensure that his restitution occurs.

8. A text cannot be judged at all if it is not readably coherent within its own syntactic framework. However, a translator may be justifiably nervous about some choices. Translators usually develop their own marking system so that they can return to trouble spots. Many translate at the typewriter to get through the first—or drudgery—draft as quickly as possible. Keeping the same pagination as the original text through Step 5 is an efficient procedure for many translators.

9. A clear record of authorial change is recorded in Anne Hébert and Frank Scott, *Dialogue sur la traduction* (à propos du "Tombeau des rois") (Montréal: HMH Limitée, 1970). Regarding self-translation, Barbara Reich Gluck, *Beckett and Joyce* (Lewisburg, Pa.: Buckell University Press, 1979), pp. 107ff., claims that Beckett writes his first "draft" in French and translates it into English for the definitive version.

10. These three inevitabilities were labelled by Eugene Nida, "Principles of Translation as Exemplified by Bible Translating," *On Translation*, ed. Reuben Brower (New York: Oxford Press, 1966), p. 13. Gerardo Vázquez-Ayora's discussion of translation levels in "La traducción de la nueva novela latinoamericana al ingles," *Babel*, 24 (1978): 4-18, reveals that many translations that are defective are effective with the reading public.

Successive translations of a masterpiece comprising, as it were, a diachronic text, show how a translator alters or follows the taste of his times, surely not always cognizant that he is adding, subtracting, or skewing. See Reuben Brower, *Mirror on Mirror* (Harvard, 1974).

11. See Peter P. Newmark, "Further Propositions on Translation: Part I," *The Incorporated Linguist* 13 (April, 1974): 34-42. He calls the translator the "second reader" and the reader of the translation the "third reader."

12. *Traduction-retour* can be carried out to establish whether the correct information has been transferred. That is, a second translator, without seeing the source text, will translate the target text back to the source language. (This is done, for example, with instructions for assembling a machine in a different language setting.) On a less crucial level, everyone has had the experience of reading a translation so eccentric that he must first figure out what the original must have been and retranslate.

Translation and Similarity

by Stephen David Ross

In what ways, in what respects, must a translation be similar to its original? Need it be similar at all? The most natural answer is that a translation ought to have the same *meaning* as the original. Unfortunately, neither meaning nor similarity of meaning is a clear notion.

Consider the possibility that a translation effectively *reproduces* an utterance in a different language. Yet a man who spoke two languages might make the same or equivalent claims in both languages, while neither would be a translation of the other. It seems plausible to conclude that in a translation, differences are relevant and important, while when a statement is simply repeated, in the same or different words, differences are irrelevant. Differences of language, circumstances, audience, and translator are important components of translation, while they are essentially irrelevant to repetition and restatement.

Consider now the case where two speakers address us in different languages. Is the statement, "The first speaker said_____" necessarily a translation, or may it be something else — a paraphrase, interpretation, or explanation? If it may be any of them, when is it a translation and not one of the others? Perhaps the more interesting question is whether we can have a translation which is not one of the others. Conversely, can we have one of the others without it also being a translation?

These are difficult questions. I will address them here in somewhat restricted terms: (a) in the context of some recent writings on meaning and interpretation; (b) in terms of the paradigm of representation, which raises similar issues; and (c) in terms of a general theory of utterance. My major concern is to show that questions of similarity of meaning severely underplay the complexities involved in the relationship of a translation to its original.

8

I.

The most natural view is that a translation preserves the meaning of the original in another language or form. It is interesting that paraphrase is distinguished from translation and that free translations are suspect: adaptations rather than translations. Both paraphrase and adaptation might well preserve the full "content" of the original. There is clearly a stronger condition for translation than preservation of meaning—preservation of form, structure, style, image, and so forth. Even in the case of a factual document, translation as against paraphrase and adaptation is constrained by demands of equivalence far beyond what would be required by the presentation of the same facts in the target language. On the other hand, translation is not restatement, where differences are minimized, but highlights certain equivalences in the context of important dissimilarities.

The approach in terms of sameness of meaning thus calls for a sufficiently general theory that would permit us to bring aspects of structure, form, image, and tone under the concept of meaning. I will later examine a general view of utterance as a basis for determining the equivalences relevant to translation. The generality of the approach will make clear the limitations of similarity of meaning as an identifying characteristic of translation as against adaptation, paraphrase, and interpretation. First, I will briefly consider three rather different views on identity of meaning which are relevant to translation.

(a) One of the strongest traditions of Western philosophy over the past few hundred years is based on the distinction between analytic and synthetic truths—the latter calling for evidence and information, the former true by virtue of meanings alone. Discussions of the distinction over the past twenty years have been overshadowed by W.V.O. Quine's article, "Two Dogmas of Empiricism," in which he argues that no adequate criterion of identity of meaning exists; analyticity, synonymy, and logical equivalence are all interrelated concepts none of which alone—and therefore, not all together—can provide an adequate foundation for understanding synonymy.[1] Quine's argument comes down in the end to the claim that synonymy and analyticity have an unavoidable element of arbitrariness within them.

It is striking that so strong a case should be made for the

arbitrariness and inadequacy of criteria of synonymy within a single language. If synonymy is arbitrary and lacks a criterion within a single natural language, it is far more deeply problematical and inadequate as a defensible notion relevant across several languages. In his more recent work, Quine has developed a theory of "ontological relativity" in which identity is language- and theory-relative. Since each language rests on different formal and theoretical constraints, both the meaning and the truth of propositions are language-relative. It follows that sameness of meaning is entirely unintelligible across different languages, and is arbitrary and indefensible within a given language.

Quine's case is relevant to synonymy of meaning taken without qualification. The natural alternative is to abandon the notion of two statements being synonymous in all respects, and replace it with the requirement that similarity of meaning be attained in some particular respects, never all. This is the approach I will take to translation.

(b) Recent work in the phenomenological tradition has produced rather similar conclusions derived from very different assumptions and methods. In *Truth and Method*, Hans-Georg Gadamer follows the development in Heidegger's early work of the thesis that all knowledge is interpretation.[2] The central concept here is of the *hermeneutic circle:* all knowledge manifests predominant contextual characteristics, location in and circumscription by the *Lebenswelt*—the field of lived experience which gives meaning to language and thought. The hermeneutic circle is generated by the contextual relativity of the interpretive dimension of knowledge, a function of the lived experience of the adjudicant-interpreter.

Gadamer's resolution of the problem of relativism affirms the importance of the hermeneutic circle. If no standpoint can be defined independent of the *Lebenswelten* of speaker and audience, the solution rests on explicitly bridging the different fields of experience. Hermeneutic method seeks to bridge the different times and points of view—the "worlds"—of speaker and audience by rendering their differences as well as their similarities explicit.

The issues highlighted by Gadamer and his critics[3] present the major alternatives for translation: *recapturing* the intentions and accomplishments of the author or *construing* his work in terms of the points of view of both author and audience. A compelling factor in support of Gadamer's position from the standpoint of translation—but relevant

10

also to history and criticism—is the continual renewal of translations of traditional texts. If recapturing the author's intentions were the goal of translation, one definitive translation of the *Iliad* would seem sufficient. Instead, we find new and different translations for every generation.

(c) In this context, George Steiner's claim that translation is interpretation is relatively modest.[4] He emphasizes the selection and choices involved in interpretation and translation that are not determined by the text, but which are a function of language, experience, and audience. In passing, I would like to emphasize that latitude in discrimination is not the same as subjectivity or relativism, nor does it involve an absence of standards.

To conclude this part of my discussion, I will identify four alternative theses defining the relationship between a translation and its original.

1. There is a unique work embedded in a text which every translation seeks to recapture—either somehow within the text to be elicited from it, or a function of the author's intentions. This is the thesis of translation identity and objectivity of interpretation. Note that translation here is interpretation, since interpretation is assumed to be capable of objective and single-valued determination.

By way of contrast, we have the following alternatives in which translation is viewed as multi-valued and variable.

2. The complexity of translation, the number of factors involved, is enormous. No translation can attain a satisfactory equivalence for every relevant factor; discretion and selection are essential to every translation, promoting variability and multiple legitimacy.

3. Translation is hermeneutical, bridging different times and worlds. There can be no definitive, objective translation, but at best one which renders explicit the different worlds of author and audience so that the work may bridge them satisfactorily.

4. Translation and interpretation are both methodic forms of utterance which stand in a many-one relation to an original. There are no criteria for specifying a single outcome in translation or interpretation relative to a given text. This latitude available to the translator-interpreter may be adjudicated by him in a variety of different ways: relative to the author's time and circumstances (alternative 1 above), relative to the audience's time and circumstances

11

(alternative 3), or in terms of whatever the translator-interpreter finds important (alternative 2). Here there is no "perfect" translation. But there may be excellent and poor translations as there may be excellent and unsatisfactory interpretations. Nothing about this alternative entails the absence of standards.

Alternative 4 is the most general and most plausible position in terms of my preceding discussion. It includes all the other alternatives in certain respects, and it is the conclusion I tend to favor. Nevertheless, there is much more to be said about some of the other alternatives. I will come back in particular to alternative 2, for there is a type of complexity that I have not yet had occasion to consider which must be included in any plausible interpretation of alternative 4.

II.

I will first develop the tension between alternatives 2 and 4 in a somewhat different way, by considering certain parallels between translation and representation rather than interpretation. Rather strikingly, recent discussions of representation in painting and the other arts have demarcated positions corresponding to alternatives 2 and 4 above. It is worth noting that even where a translation and its original are very similar—as a representation may closely resemble its object—representation and translation are neither reflexive nor symmetric relations. The original is not a translation of a translation; a work cannot be a translation of itself.

The past twenty-five years have seen a revolution in the theory of representation, largely based in the work of E.H. Gombrich and his followers. Gombrich's position is analogous to alternative 2 above concerning translation: representational art faces a difficult and complex set of selections and discriminations in the interest of veracity and faithfulness. In particular, he argues that light and color tone are often in conflict, requiring the sacrifice of one to the other.[5] M.H. Pirenne argues that perspectival realism can be attained only relative to certain positions of the spectator relative to the painting surface, and requires the sacrifice of realism to other visual perspectives.[6] The position taken by Gombrich and Pirenne is that representation seeks an equivalence with its original which is not found but created, and which involves difficult and complex decisions by the artist. It is interesting to compare such a view of representation with George Steiner's theory of interpretation and translation; both emphasize accuracy and equivalence as well as the great range of complex decisions necessary to attain such equivalence.

By way of contrast, Nelson Goodman argues in *Languages of Art* that representation requires no equivalence whatsoever, merely a set of rules and conventions for establishing denotative relations between the representation and what it represents.[7] He goes even further in some of his recent work where he argues that there is no single "way the world is," but as many ways as there are right representations.[8] According to Goodman's theory, similarity is entirely irrelevant to representation.

Goodman distinguishes representation from description on the basis of what he calls semantic and syntactic density. This distinction is embodied in alternative 4 above, divorced from Goodman's technical apparatus. A description can be neither semantically nor syntactically dense: the characters of the notational system must be finite and distinct, and its field of reference must also be finitely differentiated. There are only twenty-six letters in the Roman alphabet and each is distinct. Pictorial representations of a person, however, are infinite in number and variability of character.

Goodman has something to say in *Languages of Art* about synonymy, in particular that "two characters differ in meaning if they differ in primary extension (what that character denotes) or in any of their parallel secondary extensions (what some compound of that character denotes)."[9] Synonymy requires that *both* primary and secondary extension be preserved. He notes, however, that "as applied to natural languages, where there is great freedom in generating compounds, this criterion tends to give the result that every two terms differ in meaning."[10] Where Goodman discusses translation explicitly, he claims that "the goal is maximal preservation of what the original *exemplifies* as well as of what it says."[11] His emphasis on the importance of exemplification in translation is salutary, for we must indeed be concerned not only with the meaning of a work, but also with the kind of text of which a work or any of its components is an example. The concept of exemplification goes a long way toward handling the complexities of rich literary works. Yet the principle of maximization of both exemplification and synonymy, where differences are unavoidable, seems quite unintelligible. Nevertheless, the representation model for translation seems far more indicative of certain relevant issues than models based on synonymy or exemplification alone.

III.

I have approached translation in terms of two different models, one defined in terms of synonymy or equivalence of meaning, the other as representation. In both cases, the concept of equivalence for translation proves difficult to elucidate, and the same alternatives seem to emerge: (1) if translations are to be similar to their originals, the similarities are attained by selection, discrimination, style, convention, etc., and are not to be assimilated in any way to a copy model. The relevant factors are numerous and complex, and are not orderable according to any antecedent set of criteria. As an alternative, (2) translations may not seek any similarity whatsoever with their original, but stand in a mány-one (dense) relation with the original. Equivalences are not given by similarities, but by semantical rules and conventions. These may be implicit or explicit, colloquial, common, or created by the translator.

I am not prepared to choose between these alternatives as they stand, though I incline to the latter with suitable qualifications. I believe Goodman has made a striking case against similarity for representation, and that the same case applies to translation. The translator seeks to convey the *same meaning* in a new language as is found in the original. Not only must he choose among the various respects in which similarity of meaning is to be preserved; this is less a sameness in any particular respect, and is more an equivalence satisfactory to the constraints which govern his work. I have elsewhere called these equivalences "practical."[12] I will explain why. I will begin by developing a complexity relevant to translation which has been neglected to this point, and which has not commonly been thought relevant either to translation or representation.

I must introduce three interrelated concepts: *judgment* (or utterance) and its different modalities, *articulations* and *query*. I will begin by taking judgment or utterance in an extremely general sense, following certain of the categories developed by Justus Buchler in *Toward a General Theory of Human Judgment*.[13] Buchler follows the classical distinctions among saying, doing, and making by regarding each of them as a mode of judgment: assertive, active, and exhibitive. Each is a

14

mode of judgment insofar as it involves selection, appraisal, discrimination, and validation. I will emphasize the last. Every judgment involves a selection from alternatives that, implicitly or explicitly, is concerned with validation.

I will not take up the question here of whether every human product ought to be considered an utterance, but will simply equate utterance with validational production. Buchler's point is that judgment is a very general category, and it inhabits at least three modes which are distinguished by different methods and criteria of validation. Nevertheless, they are never to be found pure and separate, without admixture. Buchler's theory of judgment depends on two main principles: (a) that there are many modes of judgment, and (b) that each mode is pervasive throughout judgment. The first principle involves a rejection of the primacy of any particular mode of utterance. Each mode is as much concerned with validation as any other, in its own way, and cannot be replaced by another. The second principle asserts that every judgment can be given any modality: an assertive utterance, concerned as such with truth and falsity, may be regarded as an act performed by the author or as an exhibitive judgment concerned with shaping materials as such; an active judgment may legitimately be regarded as an implicit assertion about conditions and consequences or as a shaping of events and materials; an exhibitive judgment may legitimately be regarded as a statement about conditions and materials or as an act performed by an agent. It does not follow from the pervasiveness of each mode of utterance that the modes are indistinguishable.

If we take common spheres of controlled, methodic utterance such as science or art—Buchler calls them "query"—the most typical paradigm is that of speaker and audience: the audience responds judgmentally to judgments by the author. Such a relation of utterance to utterance—leading to further utterances—Buchler calls "articulation." What I wish to emphasize is that the author-audience model involves pairs of judgments with diverse modalities. The original judgment may have at least three modes; the articulating utterance may also have at least three modes. There are then at least nine pairs of judgments in such articulative contexts. Moreover, there is no justification for the articulating utterance to have the same modality as the original. A biographer may regard a scientific theory as an active judgment reflecting its author's life and experience. A psychoanalyst may regard a work of art as an expression of psychic life, both active and assertive.

In the case of translation, we have triads rather than pairs: original, translation, audience. I have noted that articulation need not generally preserve the modality of an original utterance. The question may be considered again from the standpoint of translation: should a translation preserve the modality of its original? Here again the answer must be negative, or at least greatly qualified. There are two reasons for this, one of which may seem somewhat perverse. I call attention once more to the principle that every mode of utterance is all-pervasive. Because of this, we cannot speak of articulating an assertive judgment by one which is not assertive—for every utterance is assertive. We can only speak of emphasis and predominance in a particular articulative context. A scientific report is predominantly an assertive utterance. A translation of it might be supposed also to be predominantly assertive, and under most conditions would no doubt be so. Suppose, however, a scientific thesis is set forth in elegant and persuasive prose, a translation in a pedestrian equivalent. This is a poor translation in one respect and an acceptable one in another. My point—the second reason for modal variance—is that translation can only be successful in certain respects, never all. This is the conclusion reached after parts I and II of this paper. Here, however, I am emphasizing the complex modalities of utterance. Every translation is in an articulative context involving twenty-seven possible triads of utterance, each of which is legitimate. A translation of a poem may preserve the assertive content of the original at the sacrifice of tone and structure. But a poem may also be employed as evidence of the character of its author. We may legitimately articulate any utterance with any modality by an utterance with any modality. It follows that a translator is faced in every case with a selection of modes he will emphasize, given that he cannot emphasize them all; and he may interpret the original utterance in any modality. A translation that preserved the assertive content of a scientific statement but made its rhetoric useless to a biographer seeking to understand the influences and impulses of the scientist-author would not be a successful translation in that respect. A translation of Kepler that sacrificed his argument and evidence to his Platonistic rhetoric would be unsuccessful in that respect, if not in other important respects.

The complexity of judgmental modalities leads to parallels with each of the alternative theses discussed above. Following alternative 1 is the hypothesis that there is a single translation which most completely captures the original—in this case, a translation with the same range and hierarchy of modalities. Such an assumption is dubious in terms of the modal complexity of utterance and articulation, but far more important, it is based on the assumption that translation is a repetition of the original, not its articulation. However, repetition is not translation; translation is articulation through further utterance. The differences between the utterances are essential. Every utterance may be articulated by utterances with other modalities, even in translation.

The second thesis is that judgmental modality is of indefinite complexity, and that a translation can attain modal equivalents only in some respects, not in all. This principle may be supplemented by the further proviso that translation involves selection and discrimination for a purpose and to an end, and that the modes emphasized are a function of the aims of the translation as well as the character of the original.

This gives us the third thesis, that a translation bridges the two worlds of audience and author, and that only an interpretive translation which makes explicit the two worlds and their antecedent commitments can fulfill a communicative, hermeneutic function. This principle must be supplemented by the observation that there is a third relevant world, that of the translator. Translation does not mediate transparently between author and audience, but is itself articulative and judicative. Thus, a triad of interpretive possibilities are relevant for the hermeneutics of translation.

Finally, corresponding to the principle that interpretation stands in a many-one relation to its text there is the principle that translation also stands in such a many-one relation, and that no criteria exist for distinguishing which of many competing translations is correct. This is equivalent to the principle that there is no basis for determining that a translation is superior in all respects. Translations, like interpretations, may be better in some rather than other respects, and for different purposes. Likewise, there is no correct articulation of another utterance, but articulations more or less valid according to different ends, more or less valid in different respects.

I do not want to equate translation with either interpretation or articulation, for translation is but one form of articulation. Rather, I suggest that translation is a form of articulation which emphasizes equivalences in the context of highlighted and relevant differences. It is also like representation in this respect. Nevertheless, a representation which maintained no equivalences whatsoever with its original would be no representation, however conventional or functional the equivalences might be. Goodman's case is that there are no general and stipulatable modes of similarity for representation. Likewise, there are no general forms of similarity required for translation—including modal similarities. Yet translation strives for equivalences of some sort, and is that form of articulation which emphasizes such equivalence. A translation is an articulating utterance that purports to be equivalent with its original in certain respects, despite certain fundamental and important differences—and is a translation in virtue of both equivalences and differences. Commonly, we expect translations to be equivalent in both meaning and kind to their originals—but only in certain respects, in terms of certain ends, and by means of certain essential differences.

One utterance articulates another by modifying or reinforcing some of its traits and their ramifications. There can be implicit and unintended articulation, as a poet betrays the influence of his predecessors, and there can be articulation without explicit equivalence or interpretation—for example, by reflection and departure. Nevertheless, for an utterance to be articulative, it must maintain certain equivalences with the original and must interpret it in certain respects, however covertly and implicitly. Interpretation and judgmental equivalence here are complementary. Nevertheless, neither may be explicit, overt, or intended. Interpretation has colloquially been broadened in meaning to include its overt forms. Translation has not. Still, in principle, the complementary relation of judgmental equivalence and departure is clear for all articulative utterances. We may call the equivalence component of articulation "prototranslation."

Nevertheless, where articulation is explicit—and with it translation and interpretation—different explicit roles become manifest. There can be no interpretation without implied equivalences, thus proto-translational equivalences which are not yet explicit. But wherever there is translation, there are overt differences that belong to the sphere of interpretation. When do articulative equivalences become explicit translation? Not merely where different languages are concerned, but wherever equivalence is both predominant and overtly emphasized in the context of essential differences. There are two ways in which this equivalence may be emphasized: by *asserting* the equivalence, i.e., implicitly or explicitly claiming that the articulating utterance may be substituted for the original in certain respects; and by *certifying* the equivalence. The latter is the stronger condition, and is the defining condition of explicit translation. Thus, there can be articulative interpretation where there is an implied claim of equivalence, but we do not call this translation until we are given overt guarantees. A translation calls our attention to certain essential differences of language or context but certifies that it may be substituted for the original, despite the differences, in certain respects and for certain purposes.

There remains the question of what kind of equivalences are required in translation and interpretation. I have rejected modal equivalences as not always legitimate and justified. The only plausible conclusion is that what are required are *practical* equivalences, relevant to certain aims and conditions of utterance viewed as activity. In this respect, translation is always a form of active utterance in addition to the other modalities it possesses.

IV.

I have examined several alternatives for construing the relationship of equivalence between a translation and its original. By regarding both the original and the translation as utterances, and the translation as an articulation of the original, I have suggested three conclusions: First, that the relationship of translation to original involves a minimum of nine pairs of modalities, twenty-seven triads if we include audience judgments. I have argued further that there is no basis for demanding that the modalities of the translation be identical with the modalities of the original. Indeed, I have presented three relevant principles: (a) Every judgment may be given any modality depending on articulative purposes and conditions. It follows that no criteria of preference are legitimate for all modes of articulation or translation.

(b) The complexity of utterance and its modalities requires the translator to choose among modalities as part of his translation process, and no particular mode of selection can be said to represent the original most precisely. Another way of putting this is that because of the complexity of utterance and articulation, a translator can attain certain equivalences only at the expense of others. (c) The translation process, like all articulation and interpretation, stands in a many-one relation to its original, establishing virtually an infinite range of choices for the translator in which he may (in a particular respect) satisfactorily translate the original. This is true for all originals and translations, though it may be emphasized where the original is a work of art, for in this case, the translation may also be a work of art.

Second, translation and interpretation are not so much equivalent as two closely related dimensions of explicit articulative utterance. Translation is where the equivalences necessary to interpretation are made explicit; interpretation represents the range of articulative latitude. However, there is always equivalence and inequivalence in the articulation of utterances.

Third, I have suggested that the equivalences provided by translation are practical equivalents (or substitutes) for the original enough like it for the purposes at hand. Here it seems appropriate to repeat the definition I have proposed elsewhere:

A translation is the articulation of a judgment in another language or form, or for other conditions and circumstances, with the following properties:

a. It is an active judgment to the extent that it provides a practical equivalent of the original judgment and its modalities relative to the translator's circumstances (or for the translator's audience), at least in certain respects;

b. It is an active judgment to the extent that it certifies that the translation preserves such practical equivalences;

c. It is an assertive judgment to the extent that it implicitly asserts that it preserves such practical equivalences;

d. It is a judgment of whatever modality is appropriate to such practical equivalence.[14]

The last principle incorporates whatever modal equivalences are required by the relevant conditions of articulation. Usually these are of considerable importance and influence—for example, where the translation of a bill of lading must include the same items, the translation of a court proceeding the same testimony. Assertive and exhibitive equivalence are often of major importance in translation, but not always; for example, the translation of a poem may be used to indicate biographical influences more than artistic qualities, or the rhetoric of court testimony may be sacrificed to content and mood.

Principles b and c are unvarying conditions of translation; all translations implicitly certify their accuracy in certain respects and testify to that accuracy. More precisely, all explicit and overt translations meet condition b, certifying their practical equivalence to the original. All translations, implicit and explicit, meet condition c, asserting that they are so equivalent. The certifying claim is clearly stronger since it introduces degrees of culpability. Principles a and d are variable with conditions, with translators and audiences. The latitude of discrimination and selection in translational articulation is given by these two conditions. Nevertheless, all four principles are intrinsic to all translation.

Finally, translation is by this analysis shown to be a primary form of utterance and articulation in which discrimination and selection are always constitutive factors. Indeed, intentional articulation and utterance are manifestly inventive and validational, plural in their achievements and ramifications. The requirement that translations be similar to their originals is a condition of all articulation, not to be fulfilled in any particular respects, but pregnant at all times with alternative realizations to be attained, as in representational art, by invention, creation, and discrimination, a profound manifestation of human capacities.

NOTES

1. W.V.O. Quine, "Two Dogmas of Empiricism," *From a Logical Point of View* (Cambridge: Harvard University Press, 1953). See also Quine's *Word and Object* (Cambridge: MIT Press, 1960) and *Ontological Relativity and Other Essays* (New York: Columbia University Press, 1969).

2. H-G. Gadamer, *Truth and Method* (New York: Seabury, 1975), ed. and trans. Garrett Barden and John Cumming.

3. E.D. Hirsch, *Validity in Interpretation* (New Haven: Yale University Press, 1967).

4. George Steiner, *After Babel* (New York: Oxford University Press, 1975).

5. E.H. Gombrich, *Art and Illusion* (New York: Pantheon Books, 1960).

6. M.H. Pirenne, *Optics, Painting and Photography* (Cambridge: Cambridge University Press, 1970).

7. Nelson Goodman, *Languages of Art* (Indianapolis: Hackett, 1976).

8. Goodman, "The Way the World Is," *Review of Metaphysics*, 14 (1960): 48-56.

9. *Languages of Art*, p. 205n.

10. Ibid.

11. Ibid., p. 60.

12. "Translation as Judgment," *Translation in the Humanities*, ed. M.G. Rose (State University of New York at Binghamton, 1977).

13. Justus Buchler, *Toward a General Theory of Human Judgment* (New York: Columbia University Press, 1951). See also his *Nature and Judgment* (New York: Columbia University Press, 1955) and *The Main of Light* (New York: Oxford University Press, 1974).

14. "Translation as Judgment," pp. 13-14.

Theory for Translation

by Joseph F. Graham

Suddenly, and almost as if it were somehow by surprise, there appears to be no adequate theory for translation. At least George Steiner announces as much in his survey of various claims already on file. Once considered, the surprise is hardly surprising in itself, for many others, long before and soon after, reached the same conclusion, though with more caution and rather less commotion.[1] Surely the best reason to propose any theory, after all, is that we have none. Steiner argues this to be the case and the cause, and five years after his announcement, the case has not substantially changed. What seems to surprise the most is the fact that, until recently, translation has not received the attention due its theory, despite the generality and familiarity of its practice. Such neglect by right could only be as blatant as the real inordinancy of so much attention lavished in fact, and thus the complaint of inadequacy has to charge impropriety, on the grounds that there can be no adequate theory of translation without proper theory, without theory proper. Then it is the form as well as the content of the evidence from the past which serves to prove the point. Much that has been written on the subject of translation yields very little when sifted for theoretical substance because it has always been written as if spoken in the workshop. The personal anecdotes and pieces of advice may well provide some help, but certainly not the coherent and consistent theory required for translation.

According to the argument advanced along these lines, the problem of translation is theoretical in the strict sense, being a problem in and of theory: not just the right theory but the right kind of theory, which turns out to be the only real kind. The logical consequence would then be a methodological deference, since any substantial theory of translation assumes, if it does not actually presume, some formal inquiry concerning the general principles of accomplishment, the very principles which define an object and specify a method of study. Indeed, these preliminary questions about the nature and function of a theory for translation have been raised since Steiner's gauntlet. Where the main interest has merely been to argue that previous efforts have failed to produce more positive results for want of rigor in both conception and direction, the range of critical reflection has been rather severely restricted, along with the array of conceivable alternatives. If the error in the past has been to consider translation in a partial manner, attending only to immediate concerns with matters of detail, the correction now proposed is more comprehensive only because more inclusive—and it is wider, not deeper.

Here again, Steiner may still serve as an example, since his work has been nearly exhaustive in summary.[2] Having recognized in turn the wealth of practice alongside the poverty of theory, he goes on to ask fundamental and searching questions about the very possibility of a theory for translation, in asking whether, as a matter of fact, the complex act of translation should even be considered a genuine subject for theory. He does not stay long for an answer, clearly preferring to conclude with an idea from Wittgenstein that we are still able to solve specific problems of translation and yet never find a systematic method for their solution. This may very well be true, and its truth may have something to do with the admitted complexity of the task; however, this is not much of a thesis and even less of a proof, being no more than another statement about the now chronic lack of a rigorous theory for translation. It would seem to be a weak argument from despair, with no hope beyond the defeat of all vain hope in theory, and thus an argument for a new type of empiricism or pragmatism only by default, where quality and originality are being falsely claimed for quantity and novelty. What remains to be proved, one way or the other, is whether a theory for translation could be systematic in a sense different from being synthetic or syncretic.

In deciding about the nature of a theory for translation, it is naive to begin with any direct appeal to the subject itself, even though the theory is destined and designed precisely *for* translation, after all. The special object (as against the general subject) of study is not just given in advance, but produced, defined or refined at the end. Otherwise, there would be no point to the study. This is not to say or suggest that nothing is given at all. Likewise, there would be no point. In both cases, we would not have anything to seek, having nothing to learn, from either full knowledge or complete ignorance. We start with some idea of translation, but we also start because that idea is somehow not enough. We may have no more than a sense for the word, when we set out in search of a proper theory for the real thing, and yet that sense is already subject to qualification. It is not enough for theory. In this we have another sense from the start, a second sense for theory, for what would qualify as theory. This sense, like the other, may be given but hardly taken as such for a real theory, unless we could specify and justify its use in theory. Both words, "theory" and "translation," may serve their purpose well in ordinary discourse, that being their ordinary purpose, their use in ordinary discourse; nevertheless, they may require further or extended (though not necessarily different or essentially modified) service for their use in theoretical discourse according to its purpose.

It may seem no less naive to inquire about the purpose of theory for the study of something like translation, because the very idea of theory itself would seem either too obvious or too obscure for such attention. In the first case, there could be only one idea of theory, the essential idea that theory provides knowledge, and therefore a theory of translation should be no different from all the others pertaining to significant human behavior. The general purpose of theory is thought here to be relatively simple, both clear and distinct. In the second case, the purpose could be stated in the same terms and yet understood to mean quite the opposite. The problem of knowledge, of what is meant by knowledge, has no simple, single solution, when considered in the full range of its philosophical implications—psychological, epistemological, and even ontological. The only reason, then, to pursue the matter of theory in this particular case would have to be that it runs somewhere between lowly common sense and lofty metaphysics. There is enough confusion about the status of a theory for translation to warrant some investigation, but we hope, not so much as to prevent any and all clarification. It would already be an advantage to know more about the cause for confusion.

Logical reconstruction has become a relatively familiar procedure in those areas most closely associated with translation. Since the problems of language and meaning have proved so very difficult to solve, resisting various direct approaches or frontal attacks, a more circumspect strategy has been proposed and, in certain cases, applied with notable success.[3] Again, the idea is simply to postpone the construction of a theory for basic concepts until regular plans can be drawn to carry out such a project. It would seem rather foolish to proceed in any other manner, and yet this type of critical reflection has usually come late and has seldom been met with recognition, at least at first, in the development of a discipline. Thus in the scientific study of language, major work on the logical structure of linguistic theory was delayed for some time, simply because the initial, naively empirical objectives were still being pursued with blind confidence, though transformational generative grammar did finally emerge from the impasse of structural linguistics with a specific proposal to reconsider the very nature and function of theory for language.[4] The result has been something of a revolution, a turn *around* if not *over*, directing attention back to the original task of defining a proper object and devising an appropriate method for lingustics.

The example of linguistics may be thought to serve a theory for translation in different ways, some practical and empirical, others critical and methodological, but that difference itself can only be reflected in those of the latter which affectively comprehend the former. The singular advantage of a reflexive theory is that it presents a definite profile for comparison along with an exact statement of purpose which might actually specify various degrees or levels of adequacy. The radical turn in linguistics has thus provided a general frame of reference for several theories whose objectives had never been elaborated explicitly enough for any clear recognition. On the same grounds, it could be expected that a rigorous theory for translation would also include something like a practical evaluation procedure with criteria necessarily specific, though general nevertheless. The real difference between the new formula and the old recipes for translation would then appear to be quite different, not that between one theory and none, nor simply that between the more and less explicit, but essentially that between two rather separate functions of a distinction between an art and a science of translation, if only those terms would serve to clarify rather than mystify the issue of that difference.

There could be no science for language itself without some

fundamental (both inaugural and essential) distinction like that first drawn by Saussure between *langue* and *parole* or that drawn later by Chomsky between competence and performance. Despite their crucial differences, both pairs are meant to determine a definite object for linguistics in and by abstraction from the great mass of phenomena broadly designated (though hardly defined) by the terms for language in ordinary use; furthermore, they both suggest quite similar differences, such as those between system and use, code and message, knowledge and behavior. Some of these same distinctions could be applied in the case of translation, where by analogy competence would be the ability to translate and performance the activity of translating, the one being required and assumed by the other, and where the theory of translation would be a comparative grammar representing competence as a knowledge of languages in correlation. On the basis of this initial comparison, there is reason to believe that most of the confusion about the nature and function of a theory for translation could be dissolved simply by a regular use of the basic distinction between competence and performance, which would also resolve the opposition of art and science in translation. Then scientific theory and artistic practice would be closely related, though clearly independent—much like linguistics and actual speech, or more like rhetoric and persuasion, poetics and particular poems.

This type of analogy would be fully valid if it were perfectly, completely consistent, which is hardly ever the case; therefore it should be considered relevant only to a certain extent, only to the limit of its proven value. The specific differences, which modify or perhaps even falsify the inference from linguistics, become more apparent when the relation of competence to performance is compared with that of knowledge to behavior, and science to pedagogy in each instance. Generative grammar is a theory of linguistic competence which represents the tacit knowledge of an ideal speaker-hearer, but it is not a theory of performance in itself, for any actual behavior involves much more than just language in the technically restricted sense assigned to a series of rules specifying, or generating, the set of all grammatical sentences over a given vocabulary. There is then an important difference between theoretical and practical forms of knowledge of the language. The speaker-hearer knows the language in the sense that he can perform regularly in his use of it, though he does not and need not know the language in the same sense as the linguist who provides an explicit account of the system which determines that use, nor must he learn the language through study with a grammar, either pedagogic or scientific.

In the case of translation, theory and pedagogy are more clearly related, or at least more closely associated, as could already have been gathered from the traditionally empirical and practical work in the field, where understanding is generally thought to entail some special learning. Once positively conceived as such, the long-dominant trend in thinking on the subject would actually correspond to a definite type of theory, rather than a much more unlikely lack of theory; that would be a pedagogical theory, one especially designed for performance instead of competence, and so designed because the relation between the two is more explicit and direct than in the case of language itself. This is not only to say what has always been known, that translation involves more than just competence in more than one language, but also and even primarily to suggest that the specific competence required for translation is somehow different in kind as well as in degree, and further that this so-called super-competence stands in a correspondingly different relation to any performance of translation. In very simple terms, it could be argued that for ordinary language use you do not really have to know what to do but only how to do it, whereas for translation the *what* is or soon becomes the *how*, with competence turned into performance quite openly and easily.

Of course, the mere fact of tradition does not, in itself, provide either principle or reason to correlate the development of knowledge and ability for translation in any definite, definitely necessary way; without some more substantial evidence it would be only natural to dismiss the idea once again for confusing theory and practice through conflation or reduction. There is, however, another direction of interest, which though usually opposed, also suggests (and with much greater force) that no such simple separation, nor any absolute distinction, such as that of competence and performance, could ever apply to translation so as to have the decisive effect thereby achieved in linguistics. This more recent, ostensibly more rigorous enterprise is the attempt at translation by machine.[5] It is here, strangely enough, that theory and practice, knowledge and ability, appear to be inseparable if not indistinguishable, with the no less curious consequence that the theory involved should be absolutely scientific as well as resolutely pedagogic in one and the same form. The machine knows nothing, after all, and has to be taught, quite literally, everything, so that only a completely explicit theory, one leaving no implication, no supposition, and thus demanding no interpretation at all, could ever become operative for automata.

The theoretical interest of machine translation is greater at present than its practical value, which has been deflated for some time and for good reason, since it is now fairly clear that whatever the state of technology may actually be or eventually become, the real limits on the project remain conceptual, the most difficult problems being almost always those in software as against hardware. There have, however, been very positive results in spite and even because of the rather dramatic failure to develop fully automatic, high quality translation by any of the considerable means applied to the task. Working for the machine has advanced our thinking on the subject through a series of crucial experiments with the special form and specific force of theory necessary for translation. These have been thought experiments, principally based on the premise of all computation which correlates success in mechanical operation with certain theoretical conditions on program, in particular those specifying the requirements for explicit instructions. The elaboration of an algorithm adequate for translation has thus led to discovery through difficulty, as each new obstacle has opened another perspective on what was once considered to be one big problem. That original misconception has been revised into an even bigger problem for translation, that of establishing the very unity of the subject.

Translation may now be thought to comprise an indefinite or fuzzy set of somewhat similar smaller problems, quite different among themselves and thus quite difficult to relate in any one solution, or combination of solutions which would be comprehensive and yet specifically effective. There is, first, the problem at the level of language itself. The correlation of languages for translation would seem to require something like a comparative grammar, but the hope of finding anything like the regularity of one language between two languages can hardly prevail against the force of current reflection. Although few linguists continue to argue that human languages can vary arbitrarily and without limit, the others do not contend that the

29

actual differences among essentially similar languages are systematic in any way. There is, then, the familiar and necessary (because irreducible) task of finding grammatical equivalents across languages without any reasonable procedure, without recourse beyond a dictionary to an encyclopedia.[6] As such it is an impossible task, with the very same order of difficulty found in the interpretation of texts where the meaning is not specified by the grammar alone, and where as a result the range of pertinent knowledge becomes, quite rapidly and quite literally, infinite. The work of translation has yet to be limited in principle to anything less, and it would rather seem now that such a limitation has been rejected on principle.

The only problem left is all that is left, since from here on the problems multiply under pressure from the disturbing insistence attributed to that most conscientious of all bibliographers, the legendary librarian of Babel, who would not be satisfied with less than a catalog of all catalogs, including his own, that is to say: never. If we require as much of a theory for translation, our work is hardly begun, though we could always do worse than begin all over again by finally asking whether indeed translation really is a subject for theory after all.

NOTES

1. See *After Babel: Aspects of Language and Translation* (New York: Oxford University Press, 1975), especially Chapter Four; cf. Georges Mounin, *Les Problèmes théoriques de la traduction* (Paris: Gallimard, 1963), or Eugene Nida, "A Framework for the Analysis and Evaluation of Theories of Translation," in *Translation: Applications and Research*, ed. R.W. Brislin (New York: Gardner Press, 1976), pp. 47-91; see also the essays of Edward L. Keenan, Jerrold J. Katz et al. in *Meaning and Translation*, ed. F. Guenthner and M. Guenthner-Reutter (London: Gerald Duckworth, 1978).

2. See the review by Georges Mounin, "After Babel," reprinted in his *Linguistique et traduction* (Bruxelles: Dessart et Mardaga, 1976) pp. 253-60 and for what follows *After Babel*, pp. 275 and 294.

3. For an example with some initial justification, see M.A.E. Dummett, "What is a Theory of Meaning?" in *Mind and Language*, ed. S. Guttenplan (Oxford: Clarendon, 1975), pp. 97-138.

4. See N. Chomsky, *The Logical Structure of Linguistic Theory* (New York: Plenum Press, 1975), and in particular the historical introduction, pp. 1-53.

5. The most thoughful work on machine translation has been done by Yehoshua Bar-Hillel, notably, "Four Lectures on Algebraic Linguistics and Machine Translation," in his *Language and Information: Selected Essays on Their Theory and Application* (Reading, Mass.: Addison-Wesley, 1964), pp. 185-218.

6. N. Chomsky, *Aspects of the Theory of Syntax* (Cambridge, Mass.: M.I.T. Press, 1965), p. 30, and note 17, pp. 201-2.

Translation Types and Conventions

by Marilyn Gaddis Rose

The classifications of translation types are many, but essentially overlapping in scope and longstanding in tradition. Translation conventions, on the other hand, while not difficult to identify either in translation history or current practice, are both restrictive in scope and shortlived in tradition. Type and convention are related because, by and large, the type determines the requisite or expected degree of conventionality. Both are governed by the status accorded the source text *qua* text, or, as we shall discuss subsequently, by where it belongs on the autonomy spectrum.

Let us look first at the determinative types. First of all, the classifications, with one exception, are binary oppositions. The two oldest, "literal" versus "free" and "literary" versus "non-literary," while persistently decried, are still the most used, and perhaps the most useful. Literal versus free concerns the semantic, often syntactic closeness between the source and target texts. What constitutes "closeness" (or "fidelity" or "faithfulness") is as hard to define as, say, "good taste" or "well written," but like these expressions seems to have a common ground of agreement at a given point in time and space. The ground of agreement shifts as norms shift. Literalists tend to make form inseparable from content, while partisans of free translation tend to believe the same message can be conveyed in what is perhaps a radically different form. Both camps usually concede that there are qualities inhering in the linguistic conformation of the source text that call for special strategies of approximation, but they follow opposed strategies of approximation in practice. Since the strategies are likely to become controversial where belles-lettres are concerned, we find discussions of literal versus free translation often tied to the discussion of literary versus non-literary. This division is resistant to definition also. But, like literal versus free, it is used with mutual comprehensibility both by those who have never questioned the dividing line and by those who have spent their careers describing the shifting boundary. Literal versus free denotes the translation strategy, how the translation should be carried out, whereas literary versus non-literary denotes what is being translated, how the text is classified to begin with. (A layman might suppose that literary and non-literary describe the translation strategy. They could, and they often determine it, but in the profession these polarities designate the type. A non-literary translator, if successful, is probably a good stylist, but translates material that is not creative writing.)

Translation types can be classified by function also, instead of by stragegy or substance. Katharina Reiss, who uses a ternary division, makes her division on the basis of the source text—assuming that the target text will serve a closely related, if not identical, purpose. She claims that all texts are intended to be informative, expressive, or operative. An informative text (e.g., textbook, scientific report, letter of introduction) instructs. An expressive text (e.g., belles-lettres, creative writing) affects. An operative text (e.g., advertisements, political speeches, propaganda) persuades.[1] Juliane House makes a functional division also, considering the relation of the target text both to the translator and to the translation receiver. Her division is "overt" versus "covert." In overt translation the receiving reader or listener knows that the text is a translation and recognizes that it is bound to the source culture. House includes in this category not only belles-lettres and creative writing but also persuasive pieces like sermons or political speeches, whenever these would be recognized as coming from another culture. Covert translations, on the other hand, are almost accidentally in a language other than the original, for they are not bound to a specific culture. It is as if there were a single text in two (or more) languages. The receiver is usually a close counterpart of the sender. All commercial, scientific, diplomatic documents come under this heading.[2]

A sythesizing division of types has been suggested by André Lefevere, whose material is the cohesive corpus of translation theory provided by the German literary tradition since Luther. Lefevere calls the two poles "reader-oriented" translations versus "text-oriented" translation. That is, either the translation is made to accommodate the reader's expectations (which have been formed by the prevailing taste) or the reader is expected to make his taste accommodate the translation (which may run counter to the prevailing taste).[3]

All of these divisions point to the autonomy spectrum. The two poles here are source text autonomy versus target audience needs. The gradations along the spectrum mark both the translator's relation to his material and the translation's relation to its audience. The translator, we might say, can go from reverence to reference; the translation, from presentation to adaptation. The translation will have a consistent situation both with regard to its origin and its destination. At one end of the spectrum, the complete textual autonomy of the source text is observed by the respect which the translator and his culture consider its due. Respect is shown by keeping as close as possible to a lexicon of dictionary equivalence and, within Western languages at any rate, parallel positions of syntax. Implicit is the view that there is something unique inhering in the conformation of the text, something unique that has inviolable integrity. Sacred books are not always in this category. There are both implicit and explicit taboos governing the treatment of sacred pieces, from even the most alien cultures, but these are usually outside immediate connotation and usually concern mores. (Lawrence Ferlinghetti's "#3 'Sometime during eternity'" from *A Coney Island of the Mind* would be totally offensive if it had specific verse correlation to the New Testament. As it is, it is a rhythmic, sophomoric evangelical synopsis, a document of the 1950s.[4]) If the taboos are respected, scriptural translation can come, on the contrary, at the opposite far end of the spectrum: pervasive audience need.[5] A Bible translator will not use "hills" in the native language approximation if natives of the target culture have never seen them, nor would he use a native approximation of a word which would have a double-entendre in that culture. Generally, in literature, a classic for an academic audience is accorded a high degree of textual autonomy, i.e., is given veritably calque correspondence. Editing may be extensive to compensate for the strange constructions or meaningless phrases which may result. Word-for-word translation of puns, idioms, or proverbs, for example, will be explained in a footnote. Outside literature, we find a high degree of autonomy accorded to scientific and technical texts and diplomatic documents. None of these, however, will sound like translations (as a literally translated literary classic is almost bound to), for the conventions, to be discussed shortly, differ.

At the other end of the spectrum, complete adaptation occurs when the target audience would find a close or integral translation incomprehensible or unacceptable: for example, in literature, a children's version of a classic; outside literature, simplified instruction manuals. Even when the two audiences (source and target) would be composed of readers of comparable age and education, there may be political and social factors affecting not only what gets translated but also what kind of translation is made. This occurs routinely in counterpropaganda where each side mistranslates the opposition.

Both in literature and outside literature, texts usually represent some midway point on the autonomy spectrum, veering towards one pole or the other as tastes change and as the impact of the sociohistorical environment changes.

A few remarks on a corpus of effective mid-nineteenth century writing, the Marx-Engels canon, can move our discussion from types to conventions. Without intending any disrespect toward either the Judeo-Christian or the Communist traditions, we might note as translators that the Communist canon may well be at the stage that the Old and New Testaments were at the time of Justinian. Although for the persuasion of the masses, Communists may well be just as receptive as Bible translators to the use of dynamic equivalence (a shifting cultural accommodation), in official editions of Marx and Engels it is unimaginable that such adjustments will be used in the foreseeable future. On the contrary, the effort has been to find "exact" equivalences so that the texts are transferred with as little distortion as possible. Of course, this might well be the goal of any serious translation, but in comparing texts of the *Communist Manifesto* (1848) we sense the implication that there is an undisputed, historically true text. This is not the 1848 German original, but the 1872 German edition in which Marx and Engels made a few minor textual changes. They announced in the preface that they would make no more: "the *Manifesto* has become a historical document which we have no longer the right to alter."[6] In June 1883, Engels edited and footnoted the third German edition (Marx had died on 14 March 1883) and this formed the basis for the authorized English translation on which Engels collaborated with Samuel Moore. (The first English translation was made by Helen Macfarlane in 1850.[7]) However, because of the preëminence of Russia in world Communism, translators into English have often felt bound to consider the Russian translation of 1922, that of Georgei Plekhanov revised by D. Ryazanoff. In time, there may be an English translation of the *Manifesto* comparable to the King James Version of the Bible: i.e., a translation which has associations and resonances which readers cling to, although a "modern" translation(s) may be called for. It would be presumptuous for us to predict which text(s) will be the major component(s) of the diachronic *Manifesto*. The point is that it was a synchronic document to begin with, with simultaneous distribution in six languages: Danish, Dutch (Flemish), English, French, German, and Italian. More important, the initial synchronism and subsequent textual exegesis and intertextuality imply that there is a message contained which transcends or subsumes any particular language. German was simply (or not so simply!) the first medium of an Ur-text. (We shall take up the matter of language of conception shortly.)

The formulation of an equi-valent polylingual text (once operative, now informative, always covert), whatever it may mean ideologically, means linguistically the establishment of accepted, authorized, agreed-upon equivalences of conversion, recognized reciprocities of transfer. "Der Gespenst" of the opening paragraph is henceforth "spectre," not "ghost" and not "phantom." (Most English translations use this British spelling also.) A translator would not make a children's version (as has been done for centuries with biblical narratives) in which "der Gespenst" was "bugaboo." Nor, regardless of the many viable English idioms throughout the world, would a translator adapt to a local vocabulary and use "banshee" for rural Ireland. Still, it is possible that "spectre" will either get fossilized in this usage as solely the political party haunting Western European statesmen in the mid-nineteenth century, with the result that "spectre" will be withdrawn from general usage, or a competing use of "spectre" in, say, a popular fantasy fiction series or a comic strip will make it unsuitable for being kept in the *Manifesto*. The final sentence of the *Manifesto* may be encountering semantic shift. "Proletarier aller Länder, vereinigt euch!" is popularly recalled by the catchy alliteration: "Workers of the World, Unite!" Engels' approved choice was "Working *men* of all countries, unite!" (Italics mine. This is the choice of the Moscow Foreign Language

Publishing House, 1951, and the Peking Foreign Languages Press, 1972.) "Working men" is offensive to American women readers. Two American textbooks, prior to the Women's Liberation Movement, had by "mere" editing made the manifesto more acceptable by "Workingmen" (one word).[8] (Would Women's Studies have often adopted a Marxist perspective on the family if women had realized that Engels was not inviting *them* to join the movement? This is one of those unanswerable questions in the history of translation.) Martin Lawrence, in his 1928 translation that accommodated the interpretative Russian translation of Plekhanov-Ryazanoff, uses "Proletarians of all lands, unite!"[9] Whatever else this rendering does, it makes the document sound like Russian in translation. The fact is that *sub species eternitatis* the Communist corpus is newly arrived and has not had to cope significantly with language change.

Roughly speaking, the conventionality spectrum runs parallel to the autonomy spectrum and has predictable correlations with translation types. Literal, non-literary, informative, covert, text-oriented, textually autonomous—these are all categories likely to demand a high degree of conventionality. On the other hand, free, literary, expressive and operative, reader-oriented, audience-adapted—these are all categories likely to demand flexibility instead. That is, the sciences and social sciences, the industries and professions have their conventions of conversion. These systems are far from static, but they are stable. (Vital records like birth certificates or marriage licenses will probably have few changes, while some terminologies like international arms agreements will reflect change over a few years.) A translator can make an initial expenditure of time and energy to learn them and henceforth keep up with them. This is why translators need professional training in the field(s) they translate and often have a doctorate or professional degree in that area(s). House's covert translations are often characterized by a high degree of this kind of conventionality, unless—and this "unless" is crucial—the translator must adapt the material considerably for a particular audience. (One multinational corporation in upstate New York has even developed a nonverbal sign system for use in instruction manuals in nonliterate settings. Incidentally, since these receivers would be very different from the senders, yet would not be especially aware they were using a translation, we can see that House's criteria are occasionally mutually exclusive.)

Two factors, discussed indirectly up to this point, are influential: field dominance and language of conception. They frequently merge in effect; whichever country or language area dominates a field will dominate the literature (in the sense of written material) of that field and affect both its vocabulary and logic (or lexicon and grammar). This is most evident in the physical sciences, where key terms form an interlingual lexicon with one (or two) language(s) the usual matrix of discussion. Many disciplines, moreover, have adopted certain languages for their publications and conferences. This means not only that the preponderance of texts will be in the dominant language to begin with, but that texts in other languages will use the terminology of the dominant language, that even "bilingual interference" may be present in the exposition.[10] For example, even Spanish works on Latin American social problems and economic development are replete with Anglicisms. This is not necessarily a case of language imperialism; many Hispanic scholars in these fields were trained in the United States, once did their thinking in English and still use English in part of their professional activity. More dramatic are cases where a culture emerging from colonialism or cultural dependency tries to reassert its own language or, simply, eliminate gratuitous foreign loan words. The ties of language to resurgent ethnic nationalism often will complicate the translator's task. In Québecois he will encounter not just English loan words but disguised Anglicisms; in a Dutch text of Flanders, Gallicisms; in either he might encounter traces of what was once bilingual interference. The list could go on and on. Obviously, the translator should be aware of the other language(s) operating within the language of the text he is translating and be sensitive to the ways in which culture and history determine the conventions of conversion.[11]

On a harmless level, we often notice foreign advertisements of American products translated simplistically word for word—sometimes at the expense of whatever charm the jingle had, e.g., "—goûte bon comme une cigarette doit." High fashion is still linguistically dominated by French, although the industry is no longer dominated by France. Indeed, a decade ago, we would still have used *Haute Couture* in English. A translator might observe conventions scrupulously by barbarous Franglais (e.g., "Cérise and beige, ombréed and matt, make this après ensemble épatant.")

The matter is serious, even when not insidious. Whether we believe that what we think depends on the language we use for thoughts (a commonsense version of the Whorf hypothesis[12]) or that language usage and conceptualization depend on the social context of that use (a commonsense summary of the Ervin-Tripp findings[13]), all of us as translators have had the experience of being able to express something succinctly or satisfactorily in language A that we cannot express so succinctly or satisfactorily in language B, even when we may be nearly equally fluent in both languages. Of course, these resonances, associational clusters, semantic mappings, which seem to inhere in the language itself at a particular nexus of time and space are what make translation so challenging and problematical.

It may serve a purpose for French readers to recognize American products in French advertisements or for American readers to recognize the French origin of a current clothes style. Yet it would not, we should imagine, particularly have served the cause of international Communism if the *Manifesto* had been conspicuously a German document. Even a neutral document like the United Nations Charter, promulgated in Chinese, English, French, Russian, and Spanish, elicited the observation from Antoine Favre that "we would not deny that the English text has a certain priority, since the charter was conceived in that language."[14] Yet conventions, even if incomplete and awkward, help safeguard certain kinds of communication and stabilize the translation process for a given period of time.[15]

Conventions for translating literary works exist as well, but in our day, at any rate, have been accorded much more license in application. Furthermore, they have always been closely related to the prevailing literary taste, and are, hence, relative; they form, in fact, excellent indications of the history of prevailing taste.[16] For example, one convention now obsolete is "thou/thee" in rendering second-person singular or familiar pronouns (unless some artifice of anachronism is desired).[17] Another convention, usually ignored except in sonnets, is translating the French alexandrine (12 syllables) into German or English iambic pentameter (10 syllables). This loss of two syllables poses a problem to message transfer from the outset. Stefan George's *Die Blumen des Bösen*, while satisfactory translations, are more elliptical than Baudelaire's *Les Fleurs du mal*.[18] A more extreme case is Tony Harrison's *Phaedra Britannica*, a highly effective verse play on stage, in which 56 lines are needed to expose the point of expected clash, whereas Racine needed only 30.[19] Generally, the current convention is encompassing, rather than specific: although a literary work in translation may retain an aura of a foreign culture, it should read acceptably by the standards of the target audience. We are not shocked that a recent collection of W.S. Merwin's translations, representing 20 languages and more than 29 poets, should, as Merwin concedes, sound like the same voice, for our critical latitudes are large.[20]

The practical inferences to be drawn can be borrowed and rearranged from House's title: *A Model for Translation Quality Assessment.* That is, we assess our text to decide what or whether a quality model is needed. We must decide where on the autonomy to audience spectrum both our text to be translated and its translation belong. We may overrule our initial decisions while translating, but our finished translation should reflect a consistent, coherent situation with respect to its origin and destination. It should be clear to a critic how much authority is accorded to the text itself, who the readers will be (and how aware they should be that they are reading a translation). If the match of translation to reader has been made appropriately, then the readers will not be obliged, even quasi-consciously, to consider as problems any of the issues raised by translation types and conventions.

NOTES

1. Katharina Reiss, *Texttyp und Uebersetzungsmethode* (Kronberg/Ts: Scriptor Verlag, 1976), pp. 12-21.

2. Juliane House, *A Model for Translation Quality Assessment* (Tuebingen: Verlag Gunter Narr, 1977), p. 203.

3. André Lefevere, *Translating Literature; The German Tradition* (Assen, the Netherlands: Van Gorcum, 1977).

4. *New Directions* #16 (1957): 202-3.

5. Eugene Nida and Charles Tabor, *The Theory and Practice of Translation* (Leiden: E.J. Brill, 1969); John Beekman and John Callow, *Translating the Word of God* (Grand Rapids, Michigan: Zondervan Press, 1974).

6 . Harold J. Laski, *On the Communist Manifesto* (New York: Pantheon Books, 1967), pp. 111ff.; Marx and Engels, *The Communist Manifesto* (Peking: Foreign Languages Press, 1972), p. 77.

7. Laski, *On the Communist Manifesto.*

8. Samuel H. Beer, ed. (New York: Appleton-Century-Crofts, 1955), p. 46; Lewis S. Feuer, ed. (Doubleday Anchor, 1959), p. 41.

9. Martin Lawrence, trans. (New York: Russell and Russell, 1963). Mikhail Bakunin did the first Russian translation for *Kolokol* in 1863.

MARILYN GADDIS ROSE

10. Term coined by Uriel Weinreich, *Languages in Contact* (1953) (reprint, The Hague: Mouton, 1974).

11. Louis-Jean Calvet offers an extreme form of the argument in *Linguistique et colonialisme, petit traité de glottophagie* (Paris: Payot, 1974).

12. Benjamin Lee Whorf, *Language, Thought, and Reality*, ed. John B. Carroll (Cambridge: M.I.T. Press, 1956).

13. Susan M. Ervin-Tripp, *Language Acquisition and Communicative Choice*, ed. Anwar S. Dill (Palo Alto: Stanford University Press, 1973).

14. *Principes du droit des gens* (Fribourg: Librairie de droit et de jurisprudence, 1974), p. 102: "On ne saurait contester une certaine primauté au texte anglais qui est celui de la langue dans laquelle il a été conçu." It will be noticed that in order to achieve smooth English syntax I somewhat sacrificed the conceptual perspective. If I had thought the text required deference *qua* text, I would have used "One could not dispute a certain primacy to the English text which is that of the language in which it was conceived."

15. Sometimes the translation convention sounds infelicitous to begin with but becomes a new term in the target language. E.g., in contemporary critical theory, *lisible* and *scriptible* are rendered as "readerly" and "writerly." "Differance" passes into English with its deliberate misspelling.

16. André Lefevere has pointed out that translations may be used to renew a literature or as a means of attacking the literary establishment with an imported authority; "On Style in Translation," *Paintbrush*, 4 (Spring and Autumn, 1977): 7-11. Reuben Brower's *Mirror on Mirror* (Cambridge: Harvard University Press, 1974) surveys how translations of a given classic comprise veritably a diachronic work through time. Lefevere's *Translating Poetry: Seven Strategies and a Blueprint* (Assen, the Netherlands: Van Gorcum, 1975) studies Catullus #64 in seven modern English translations.

17. Compare, for example, the French, German, and English versions of Wilde's *Salomé*. In Lord Alfred Douglas' version, massively edited by Wilde, the imaginary, ahistorical Israel is enhanced by such anachronisms. Richard Howard sacrifices this effect when he translates Wilde's anglicized French into neutral American idiom, but Howard does remove the silliness of the play by this modernization. See Howard's translation in *Shenandoah*, 29 (Summer, 1978): p. 36. See also my "*Synchronic Salome*" in *The Language of the Theatre: Problems in the Translation and Transposition of Drama*, ed. Ortrun Zuber (London: Pergamon Press, 1980). pp. 146-52.

18. See Lilian Furst, "Stefan George's *Die Blumen des Bösen*: a Problem of Translation," *Revue de littérature comparée*, 48 (1974): 203-17; Margot Melenk, *Baudelaire-Uebersetzungen Stefan Georges* (München: Wilhelm Fink Verlag, 1974).

19. See my "Style in Translation," *Paintbrush*, 5 (Spring & Autumn 1978): 32-36.

20. W.S. Merwin, *Selected Translations 1968-1978* (New York: Atheneum, 1979).

Knowledge, Purpose, and Intuition: Three Dimensions in the Evaluation of Translation

by H. Stephen Straight

The effectiveness of a translation appears to be determined by three different sets of variables, or dimensions of variation.[1] First, there is the dimension of *knowledge*: does the translation exhibit adequate understanding of the cultures of both the author of the original and the intended audience of the translation? Second, there is the dimension of *purpose*: does the translation succeed in achieving the purpose defined for it by the translator? (A separate but related question is whether that purpose is or is not a worthy one.) Third, there is a dimension that I shall call, somewhat reluctantly, *intuition*: is the translation satisfying? I shall discuss each of these three dimensions in turn.

Knowledge: Cultural And Linguistic

Certainly the most obvious, and probably the most important, factor contributing to the success of a translation is the translator's knowledge. Flaws or gaps in knowledge of the linguistic system and cultural context of the author of the original will keep the translator from understanding it; similarly, successful communication with the intended audience of the translation depends upon full and accurate knowledge of their language and culture. The range of such knowledge is very great indeed (see table); few translators possess the degree of bilingualism/biculturalism necessary to be free of any danger of error along this dimension.

TABLE Outline of Knowledge Translators Must Have[2]

I. *Ecology*
    climate, terrain (desert, rain forest, mountains, etc.)

41

flora, fauna (roses, willows, rodents, wombats, etc.)
exploitation patterns (slash-and-burn agriculture, coon hunting, cave
dwelling, deep-sea fishing, etc.—overlaps with category II)
II. *Material Culture, Technology*
household objects (machetes, mackinaws, gourds, Pepsi, etc.)
housing, other buildings (chalets, teepees, etc.)
means of transportation (oxcarts, jumbo jets, snowshoes, etc.)
technical knowledge (penicillin, Polaris, poisons, etc.)
III. *Social Organization*
classes, kinship categories, sex roles (clerics, uncles, male nurses,
panhandlers, etc.)
legal, political system (headmen, electioneering, etc.)
IV. *Mythic Patterns*
cosmology (Eden, nirvana, Milky Way, etc.)
taboos (profanity, mother-in-law avoidance, body odor, etc.)
supernatural notions (ancestor worship, transmigration, etc.)
V. *Linguistic Structures*
sound system (especially important for songs or poems, but also whenever
rhyme, rhythm, or alliteration is present)
word formation (especially important when obligatory markings of
number, gender, tense, etc., are found in one language but not the other,
but also when word formations are used in the original for stylistic
purposes)
word meanings (number of near-synonyms for a given concept can differ
radically between languages; idiomatic and metaphorical expressions constitute
the most frequent and most obvious source of translation difficulties)
syntactic relations (problems arise because of such things as different
resources in regard to conjunctions and other transition markers or
and other markers of co-reference)
pronouns

It is also important to realize that the dimension of knowledge is
not simply a matter of knowing each of the two languages and cultures,
the source and the target, as well as does a "native" in each of them.
The translator must also work out all manner of equivalencies,
correspondences, and parallels *between* the two. This task requires a
keenness of insight surpassing that of most mortals. In fact, translators
(and translation critics) I have talked to confess that the task is, in the end,
an impossible one. The incommensurability of cultures and languages
cannot be denied, they say, but the skilled translator can do much to
combat it, however partial or ephemeral the victories may be.
Nevertheless, all translators must strike whatever balance they judge best
between outright substitution, whereby the linguistically and culturally

different is replaced by the familiar, and plain instruction, whereby the readers are painstakingly led to see the exotic as nearly as possible "in its own terms." Substitution runs the obvious risk of depriving the work of any hint of its cultural-linguistic origins, while instruction can rob it of whatever claims it had on spontaneity and universality. Most translations seek some middle ground wherein the foreign aspects of the original are preserved without making the reader feel that it was the product of an alien mind.

It is already clear from the discussion of the knowledge required for effective translation that the task of translation demands careful weighing of alternatives. It should also be clear that choice among these alternatives cannot be made on any absolute grounds. Rather, translators make their choices on grounds relative to the particular work at hand. It is this topic to which we now turn.

Purpose: The Final Decision Is The Translator's

Translation is the less effective of two possible ways to make a work accessible to people who are not native to the culture and language in which it was produced. The other, more effective way to do this is called foreign-language teaching (as it is practiced in most places, anyway). Whenever there exists linguistic or cultural incompatibility between a work and a particular audience, compatibility may be sought either by working changes on the work or by working changes on the audience. Translation (and other types of adaptation) puts the work into a form that is intelligible to the audience, while foreign-language teaching (and other types of education) equips the audience to understand the work in its original form.

Clearly, each of these two routes to the goal of enlarging the audience for a given work has its advantages and disadvantages. The instructional route has the great advantage of preparing the new readers to interpret the original work, and all other works deriving from that same cultural-linguistic milieu, entirely on their own. Little attention need be given to the particular work that one seeks to make accessible to the new readers except to be sure that its original audience is accurately identified. The great disadvantage of the instructional route is that its success is almost wholly dependent upon the efforts of the members of the intended new audience, who must work hard and long to acquire the skills and background knowledge needed to understand the work. Education may be more "effective" than translation, but it is by no means as efficient: the accessibility of works in other languages will grow very slowly indeed if we depend upon the motivation of readers to learn those languages.

The great advantage of translation, then, is its efficiency: the accessibility of a given work can be increased enormously through the efforts of sometimes just a single person. In fact, there are many examples of works which have many times more readers in translation than they could possibly have had achieved in their original form (consider the Bible, or the works of Hans Christian Andersen). But translation has an equally enormous disadvantage: the measures of its success, and therefore also the criteria for its performance, are extremely difficult to define.

In the previous section of this discussion, I made the point that the translator usually has a large number of alternatives to choose from in conveying the meaning of a word, phrase, sentence, or opus to people in a different cultural-linguistic group. Even if we agree that the meaning of the translation and the meaning of the original should be "equivalent"—and some might object even to that claim—we are faced with any number of ways of defining such equivalence. Surely the only way to achieve complete equivalence between the meaning perceived by the work's new readers and that perceived by its original readers is to abandon translating and take up foreign-language teaching, for the translation which is referentially faithful to the original is apt to mystify the reader through references to things which do not seem relevant (or even possible), and referential equivalence cannot hope to be an adequate criterion for the handling of idiomatic or metaphoric expressions.

Perhaps the most reasonable approach to the definition of equivalence is that of ferreting out the reaction of the readers of the original work and to seek to have the translation evoke that same reaction in *its* readers. This approach to literary criticism is often criticized as "the effective fallacy," because the reception that a work gets from its readers may not be so esthetically informed as the reception it gets from its critics. This criticism does apply here as well, I believe, and the translator must weigh carefully all decisions concerning *whose* reactions are to be included among those to be evoked by the translation. In fact, these decisions are generally made without much (or even any) explicit attention: the translator's own personal responses to the original work and to the translation-in-progress are employed as the touchstone for the translation process. To the extent that the translator's "reading" of the original matches that of other readers of the original, the translation—if it succeeds in evoking that same reaction—will be judged by such readers to be a good translation.

However, many different facets of a work contribute to any reader's reaction to it, and probably no two readers respond to the same set of facets. It follows that no translation is likely to succeed in conveying all of these facets. Therefore, the translator must decide what the *purpose* of the translation is, relative to the various purposes it might have by virtue of the myriad facets of the original. If the original is found to be musical in its use of sounds and meter, then the translator is likely to seek such musicality in the translation. If the original contains unusual folk sayings that strike its readers as fresh and original, then the translator will probably not substitute well-known proverbial equivalents for these but rather to preserve their pungency through a more "literal" rendering.

Indeed, as was pointed out earlier, the number of ways in which the translator's judgment must come to bear upon the selection of alternatives is very large, and in each case the decision between the more "literal" and the more "free" rendering must be made relative to the translator's perceived purpose. Should the translation seek to preserve the metaphoric quality of an idiom used in the original, or is that idiom too "frozen" metaphorically to be worthy of literal translation? (Surely a literal translation of the parting phrase "So long!" in English would be inappropriate, but what about an idiom such as "fly off the handle" for "lose one's temper"?) Are references to such things as occupational specialties (for example, "busboys" or "tax lawyers" or "academic deans") worth the descriptive phrases or footnotes needed to convey their referential domain to readers whose language lacks handy terms for them, or are rough equivalents (say, "helper," "adviser," or "administrator") sufficient?

Furthermore, the translator is free to (and often does) skew the translation away from trying to evoke the same response in the new readers as it does in the old. The translation may be designed to convey as much as possible of the cultural and linguistic context of the original. The extreme examples of this approach contain various exotic phrases, many passages that are supplemented with explanatory prose meant to help the readers find their way through the piece of the world depicted in the work, and numerous words that are left untranslated except for lengthy footnotes accompanying their first occurrence.

Such decisions about how "faithfully" to render the original are heavily influenced by the translator's perception of the audience for the end product. And I believe that it is by focusing upon this issue that the notion of "purpose" can be given some stable basis for use as a criterion for the evaluation of translations. Decisions about which facets of the original are to be conveyed in the translation cannot usually be made relative simply to the entire language-and-culture matrix into which it is to be placed, since not enough guidance is usually contained in this matrix for making the specific decisions that must be made. Instead, the translator must choose among translational alternatives on the basis of an informed judgment concerning the specific background knowledge, sensitivities, and motivations of the people who would be expected to read the translation. Often such a specification of the intended audience is ready at hand: a scholarly work should be translated for scholars, a children's book for children, a shop manual for mechanics. But sometimes such obvious signs are not available, and the translator must decide the matter in one way or another.

However the translator decides, some readers will be dissatisfied. Attempts to convey the metaphorical texture of the original, for example, may puzzle the reader who lacks the knowledge of the idioms or mythic patterns of the culture of the original, while the sophisticated reader will be furious if such metaphors are replaced by their rough, homegrown equivalents. But as long as we evaluate the translation relative to its intended audience, we will not do the translator any disservice.

On the other hand, we may base our evaluation of a translation not only upon whether we feel it achieves its particular purpose well or badly. We may also judge the worthiness of that purpose itself. Translating the poems of Rainer Maria Rilke into the language (and culture) of American ten-year-olds might well be judged a bad project no matter how adeptly we felt it had been done. In fact, translating

Japanese haiku into anything less than the language of orientally sophisticated readers, might reasonably be condemned: something less than that would be mere imitation rather than translation, the aficionados would say, and they would probably be right.

I have tried to reduce the problems of translation, the criteria by which we are justified in evaluating a translation, to three questions: (1) Does the translation succeed in evoking a response in its readers that is qualitatively equivalent to that of the readers of the original? More specifically, does it enable its readers to grasp as fully as they can what there is about the original that makes it meaningful, valuable, beautiful, and worth being translated? (2) Does it do so by exploiting resources in the two languages (and cultures) in a way that reflects their true commensurability? To put the same question in more negative terms, does it evoke a comparable response without unwarranted masking of differences between the cultural (and linguistic?) contexts of the original and the translation? (3) Should this translation (of this work for its intended readers) have been attempted in the first place?

It seems to me that these three questions, all of which relate to the translator's purpose in performing the translation, allow one to evaluate different translations on the same objective grounds. Having identified the intended audience of a given translation, one has some basis for gauging the extent to which members of that audience would be optimally served by the translation as a means of coming as close as they could to experiencing what readers of the original do (or did). The goal of translation, now made openly dependent upon the limits and motives of its intended audience, could thus be seen to allow for a wide range of quite distinct but equally "good" translations of a single work, each directed at a different audience or achieving its effects by different but equally effective means. In each case one would be able to support one's critical evaluation with explicit reference to aspects of the culture and language of the original and of the receiving audiences. To be sure, critics would still have ample room to disagree with one another about how to specify the criteria to be employed in any particular instance. What is the best gauge of the original force of the work that has been translated? Was the original audience sub-group A or sub-group B of the author's culture? Should the translator of a non-contemporary piece of literature write for today's audience or for the audience contemporary with the original (e.g., should Schiller be rendered in eighteenth-century English)? If a translation seems to have strengths that are greater than or different from those of the original should we call it an "adaptation" rather than a translation? These and other such questions are not likely to be answered with unanimity, but at least the grounds for disagreement should be fairly clear, and open to discussion.

Intuition: Inherently Unverbalizable Factors In Language Use

Translation is a skill, but it is also an art. The factors of knowledge and purpose that have thus far been identified clearly belong to the realm of skill: an attentive and industrious bilingual should, it would seem, be able to take all of these factors carefully into account and thereby succeed in crafting a translation that would meet with critical approval. But what about translation as an art? Does our esthetic response to a translation lend itself to treatment in the same way as the other responses that have been appealed to here, or will some translations simply seem better than others in ways that are beyond scientific investigation? Certainly those who believe in the irreconcilability of science and art would say that there is simply no accounting for esthetic judgments in scientific terms. I think they are wrong, at least in principle—although they may be right in practice, for our present ignorance of the bases of language use is too great for anyone to feel terribly sure of himself in accounting for it scientifically. Nevertheless, I firmly believe that a crucial breakthrough in our understanding of the psychological basis for language abilities has been made which promises to revolutionize our conception of the putatively "ineffable" factors in creative language use.

The breakthrough I refer to concerns the role of the right hemisphere of the brain in language. Long believed to be merely the "minor" or "nondominant" half of the brain, the right side of the cortex has recently been shown to have capacities that its "major" or "dominant" opposite partner lacks.[3] To be sure, a normal person who is deprived of the use of the left hemisphere (through injury, disconnection, or other impairment) does lose the ability to express thoughts in words. However, such a person retains, through the activities of the right hemisphere, full capacities in the realm of visual spatial perception and action plus some degree of simple language comprehension. More importantly for the present argument, compar-

48

able impairment of the *right* hemisphere, leaving the left hemisphere intact, leads to no obvious loss of abilities of linguistic expression and reception but to clear disabilities in the realm of visual and spatial processing, including spatial orientation, face recognition, and other such "nonlinguistic" activities. Moreover—and here is the point that I believe to be crucial—the person with solely left-hemispheric language abilities (that is, the person deprived of normal left-and-right cognitive processing in language performance) does, in all accounts, exhibit a general "cognitive deficit"[4] that shows up in such impairments as distractability, disorientedness, and inability to engage in lengthy abstract discourse.[5] These debilities have thus far generally been attributed to the loss of strictly nonlinguistic faculties, and the various imaginal, inferential, and motivational deficits this loss might cause. What I propose (though this is admittedly a claim which can have its validity neither demonstrated nor rejected on the basis of current neuropsychological research findings) is that language does in fact involve both hemispheres, with the right hemisphere providing the basis for those aspects of language processing that are more global and holistic than the more sequential and segmental aspects governed by processes of the left hemisphere.

The import of all this for the evaluation (and the composition) of translations is that many of the decisions made by the translator (as well as by the original author) may well be influenced by an essentially "intuitive," right-hemispheric mental apparatus that is simply not included in our curent linguistic models. Furthermore, it may be that the factors to which the right hemisphere is sensitive will continue to defy explicit rational analysis because they are, by their very nature, unavailable for recognition or manipulation by the compartmentalizing, sequencing, and bracketing operations of the left hemisphere, upon which we depend for the logical classification and explanation of events. The "right brain," in other words, may only be able to express itself in ways that will elude objective study. So that the author's decisions as to what to include in the original work and also the translator's decisions as to how to translate these may be based upon factors that are not only unnamed but unnameable!

On the other hand, fairly recent developments in the analysis of discourse show some promise of getting beyond the level of the word and the sentence to the level of narrative and interactive language.[6] There is yet some chance that the "inherently unverbalizable" may succumb to scientific investigation (though current approaches to discourse continue to employ essentially linear, dissecting models of language which, if my argument here is correct, will have to give way to more multidimensional, holistic models).

In any case, this contribution of the right hemisphere might well account for a good measure of our current inability to provide logical, neat explanations for our judgments that this or that word, line, phrase, or paragraph is better or worse than its translational alternative. Like composition and translation, evaluation too may sometimes be based upon Gestalt-like, part-to-whole judgments that are simply not tied to discrete elements within the text being evaluated. Until we know a great deal more than we do now about the processes which underlie language use, we shall simply have to accept the fact that there is an essentially "intuitive" component in our evaluation of translations, a component that lies outside and beyond the more familiar and discernible dimensions of knowledge and purpose which have been described in the first two sections of the present discussion.

NOTES

1. In an earlier paper I discussed translation from a variety of standpoints: cultural, linguistic, psychological, and practical. Upon reflection, it has become apparent to me that *evaluation* of the quality of translations was the implicit topic of that paper, which sought to identify the attributes of intellect, will, and judgment that characterize the "effective translator." (See "Translation: Some Anthropological and Psycholinguistic Factors" in *Translators and Translating*, ed. T. Ellen Crandell [SUNY-Binghamton, 1975], reprinted in *Translation in the Humanities*, ed. M.G. Rose [SUNY-Binghamton, 1977].) The aim of the present paper is to reconsider and elaborate upon the content of the earlier paper with this issue of how to evaluate translations clearly in the foreground. I am grateful to the University of Ghent for enabling me to present the penultimate version of this paper to an audience there, 17 December 1979, and especially to F. J. Vandamme and R.A. Young for their helpful commentary on that occasion.

2. Largely after E.A. Nida, "Linguistics and Ethnology in Translation Problems," *Word*, I (1945): 194-208.

3. Robert Ornstein, *The Psychology of Consciousness* (San Francisco: William Freeman, 1972); see also Stephen D. Krashen, "Cerebral Asymmetry," in *Studies in Neurolinguistics*, II, H. and H.A. Whitaker, eds. (New York: Academic Press, 1976), 157-91.

4. A.R. Luria, *Higher Cortical Functions in Man* (New York: Basic Books, 1966).

5. J. Eisonson, "Language and Intellectual Modifications Associated with Right Cerebral Damage," *Language and Speech*, 5 (1962): 49-53.

6. William Labov, "The Transformation of Experience in Narrative Syntax," *Language in the Inner City* (Philadelphia: University of Pennsylvania Press, 1972), pp. 354-96; D.N. Sudnow, ed., *Studies in Social Interaction* (New York: The Free Press, 1972).

Beyond the Process:
Literary Translation in
Literature and Literary Theory

by André Lefevere

For a long time the only translations deemed worthy of study have been translations of literature. This approach originated in the eighteenth century and tended to dominate the field until about the second decade of the twentieth. As a result, the study of translations was limited to esthetic evaluation of translations of literature and of the various ways in which various languages were or were not able to express certain concepts.

Towards the end of its reign, this type of study also branched out into linguistic philosophy and linguistic psychology. The reaction against this approach, which is still fairly widespread in the field today, has made the study of translation (by which is usually meant the study of the translation process) almost exclusively a province of linguistics, without, however, being able to profit to any great extent from the methodological innovations that have characterized linguistics over the past few decades. In the typical linguistics-oriented study of translation some lip service is usually (almost ritualistically) paid to literary translation, but this serves more often than not as an excuse to skip the problems connected with that particular type of translation and to move on to what are considered the "real" issues. As a rule, this type of investigation has very little to say that transcends the platitudinous about the translation of literature.

This state of affairs is all the more regrettable since current literary theory—to which the study of literary translation is more often than not referred by linguistic endeavors in the field—does not seem to have all that much use for translation either. There are a number of reasons for this. Translation is obviously not a problem as long as the study of literature is equated with the study of one national literature. It becomes both necessary and problematic as soon as one enters the domain of literary theory and comparative literature. To the founding fathers of comparative literature translation was, essentially, a scandal, a rather unpleasant reminder of the limitations imposed on the new discipline by human imperfection: something one would stoop to, or at least allow one's students to stoop to, only under cover of great secrecy. The situation has obviously changed since then, especially in North America, but we are still faced with a certain residual smugness about "mere" translations on the part of those engaged mainly in the study of national literatures, compounded by a residual feeling of guilt, or at least uneasiness, on the part of many comparatists. It is clear that these attitudes are explicable only in terms of an essentially romantic theory of literature which tended almost to equate the literary work of art with the language in which it was written. The genius of language X, speaking through finely frenzied poet Y was, if I may be allowed a slight oversimplification, the basis of all literary creation. As soon as one is ready to admit that the literary work of art is also composed of nonlinguistic elements, genre, for example, the whole question of (un) translatability, along with the smugness and the guilt, is seen in a new and much less problematic light.

Recent literary theory has, for the most part, been avowedly ahistorical. Since the part played by translations in a literature is mostly connected with the historical evolution of that literature, this kind of theorizing could do little more than pass over translation in silence, or treat it with a neglect that has by no means always been benign in nature.

Furthermore, linguistic approaches to translation have, as has been indicated above, tended to focus almost exclusively on the study of the translation process, even though they had to admit at the same time that they were doing so against great odds, since the actual process is unobservable and has therefore to be reconstructed speculatively on the basis of the comparison of two products. No wonder the current vogue of process-studies (which should also be seen in the historical perspective of the great wave of—admittedly shortlived—enthusiasm for machine translation) has never really succeeded in producing models that left the vague, the trivial, or both all that far behind. As a result, many scholars in the field are becoming increasingly disenchanted with the proliferation of attempts to formalize and schematize what cannot really be formalized, not in any way that goes much beyond the intuitive knowledge of the process which practising translators keep stored in their heads.

This is most emphatically not to say that I believe that the translation process should not, still less that it cannot, be taught. I simply want to submit the opinion that the most profitable way to teach it is not by means of models, which tend not only to become increasingly abstract, but also to exhibit a drift to what I would like to call "semantic terrorism," the devious process during which the model constructor forces his or her reader to invest heavily in trying to familiarize himself/herself with the jargon used by that constructor, only to find that the conclusions drawn by the model constructor might be (and in many cases actually have been) reached without this dubious expenditure of time and energy.

It is my opinion that knowledge of the translation process is, in fact, "personal knowledge," the kind of knowledge that can be transmitted only by actually working with somebody who has given proof that he or she possesses it. Ideally this kind of knowledge would be most profitably transmitted in private tutorials, in which both instructor and learner would tackle the same text. It is true, of course, that the instructor does, in this type of situation, work from an implicit model. My contention is merely that this kind of model does not gain from being made more explicit and being presented in what amounts to a void, abstracted from the living questioning and response in the concrete tutorial situation.

As this personal knowledge is transmitted, it will, I believe, soon become obvious that there is in fact no difference at all between the transmission of specifically "literary" and specifically "non-literary" or "pragmatic" translation skills. All translators have to know much more than the languages they work with, if they are to make a good, or even passable, job of their translations. The "more" a translator of literature has to know does not, in my opinion, set him apart from the translator of, say, works on biochemistry, who also has "more" to know. After all, we do not distinguish between "pragmatic" translations on the one hand and "biochemical" translations on the other. It would therefore seem that the special status of "literary" accorded to certain translations is, essentially, negative in nature. Labelling a translation "literary" has, in the past forty years, been tantamount to excluding the class of translations of which it is part from further investigation into the translation process; this exclusion is not necessarily because of any malice or philistinism, but simply because models are most easily constructed on the basis of texts which, obviously, lend themselves more easily to model constructing. Translations of literature have been carefully kept outside this vicious circle.

It would therefore seem more profitable if we approached the specific nature of literary translations (or translated literature) on the level of the product, and not on that of the process, where its specificity is not all that apparent. We should, in other words, concern ourselves with the various ways in which translated literature functions in the wider context of the target literature. It is here, too, that the study of translated literature can make a distinctive (and distinguished) contribution to literary theory.

In order to make this clearer I shall have to resort to a brief digression about the "polysystem hypothesis." The term "polysystem" for the description of a literature has been extrapolated from the writings of the Russian Formalists by Itamar Even Zohar, and taken over by other members of the so-called Low Countries group.[1] The term "polysystem" denotes that a literature is never, at any moment in its history, the monolithic whole which textbooks tend to present it as, but rather, in each phase of its evolution, a collocation of different, often antagonistic, trends, dominated by the set of literary works a given era accepts as "canonized." This canonized literature comes under attack from other trends, which try to displace it and achieve canonized status themselves. Analogously, one literature can occupy a canonized position vis-à-vis another. The most striking example, of course, is that of classical literature vis-à-vis all the literatures of Europe in the Renaissance. Here again, canonization is by no means final and irreversible. Up to 1750, for example, French literature was considered the canonized ideal most German writers aspired to, a situation radically reversed some fifty years later.

The polysystem hypothesis also holds that the dynamic nature of literary history can best be appreciated if individual works are read against the background of what is usually referred to as an "inventory of literary procedures," including genre, theme, plot, allusion, quotation, the natural language in which the work is written, etc. This inventory, which changes and develops all the time, is, as it were, an a priori of literature: individual procedures migrate from one literature to another, flourish in one, do not "take" in another, are left in abeyance, sometimes for centuries—witness the fate of the genre called "tragedy"—to be revived and abandoned again.

Finally, the inventory does not change in a vacuum. Following Pavel Medvedev,[2] the polysystem hypothesis holds that the literary polysystem is part of the "ideological milieu" of a given era. What apears in the ideological milieu may profoundly affect the literary polysystem, not just in the case of subject matter—Darwin's theory of evolution and its repercussions in Tennyson's *In Memoriam*, to quote an obvious example—but also in the case of genre, as when the abolition of the Imperial Examination after the Mongol Conquest of China created a class of unemployed (and unemployable) scholars, who were forced to make their living by dramatizing the classical novels. In the process, they created Chinese drama, the lyrical interludes of which later became independent as a lyrical form in their own right.

Translations of literary works are often used as weapons in the struggle between the canonized and non-canonized tendencies within the polysystem, a struggle which is often a matter of prestige. By the very fact of its canonization, the reigning trend in the polysystem possesses great prestige at a given time—great enough, it would seem, to overshadow most, if not all challengers. The latter's problem is to produce literary works that are equally prestigious in support of the alternative poetics they propose. Almost by definition, these works will not be found inside the reigning literature. They will therefore have to be imported from outside the polysystem. This strategy not only confers prestige, but also relative immunity: the foreign work, having been produced outside the native polysystem, cannot really be judged by native standards, precisely because it presents an alternative to them.

It is interesting to note, in this context, that the polysystem hypothesis alone can make sense of the many pseudo-translations that tend to be published when the canonized branch of literature does not produce "great works" any longer, but when critics who act as its apologists do, nonetheless, rigidly stick to its principles, as in late neoclassical France, for example, or late Augustan England. Chatterton, MacPherson and others (most noticeably Horace Walpole in the novel) tried to bestow respectability on their alternative poetics by claiming—somewhat paradoxically at first sight—that it had its roots in a long and venerable tradition, "unjustly" (how could it be otherwise?) forgotten. Similarly, to quote a final example, Ezra Pound enlisted classical Chinese poetry in the militant cause of Imagism.

Translations, then, are produced, often by those who tend to think of themselves as writers rather than critics or theorists, not only to make a foreign work available within their own literary polysystem, but also as a contribution to the cause of an embattled (or even victorious) literary trend. Hence, of course, the many and radical fluctuations of style in this type of translated literature. There is, however, another kind of translator of literature, those who do not produce translations for the dual purpose mentioned above, but simply to make foreign works available, to give readers who are not familiar with the language of the original the materials needed for their own concretization of the text. Ideally, their mental constitutions display the "union of translator and literary scientist, of recreative artist and universally educated scholar."[3] They, in other words, know the "more" a translator of literature has to know, whereas the first type of translator often does not, or to a very fragmentary extent only. To my mind their work is both more valuable and more scientific than that of critics, since they simply make readings of the work possible, without offering any readings of their own (even though, as with the model, a reading is implicit in the choices they make in their translations), thereby keeping their distance from the wilder fringes of polyinterpretability.

There is also, to complete this unholy trinity, the literary theorist who is interested in the contribution which the study of translated literature is able to make to the study of literature in general. His or her task is most emphatically not to "rule" on the quality of existing translations—an activity which, when undertaken at all, is often left to self-proclaimed arbiters, as often as not in the service of a certain type of poetics, who self-righteously proceed to damn whatever does not agree with their poetic concept. Rather, the literary theorist attempts to describe the way in which texts calling themselves translations function in the target literature. In trying to do so, he or she is faced with a number of problems which, in turn, open up virtually virgin fields of research. What foreign works are translated "into" a literature at what time, in the service of what poetics? This, incidentally, leads to the compilation of a kind of "historical poetics" of translation, a compendium of strategies used by translators in the past, which may be used again by future translators or at least hint at possible solutions for certain problems on the process level. What is the pressure (if any) of the ideological milieu on the translator? In other words, what "mistranslations" is he or she forced to make? In what way does a translation attempt to influence the ideological milieu of the target culture, and what does this mean in terms of the translation strategies used (the King James version of the Bible, for example, versus the *Good News for Modern Man* approach). What repercussions do translated works from other sectors (political, religious, economic) of the ideological milieu have on the literary polysystem? In other words, what does Sir Richard Burton, for example, want to achieve when he says in the introduction to his Catullus translation that he has tried to bring out the pederastic elements in the original? How do individuals, as individuals or as representatives of groups, concretize or "receive" certain literary works of art? Translation seems, in this respect, to be an almost foolproof basis for the study of reception aesthetics.

Does the trend in translating in certain countries and at certain times amount to the equivalent of a cultural policy? For example, many newly independent nations are trying to strike a balance, in selecting their canonized works, between local work and foreign imports, and in the case of the Soviet Union, the different national literatures are systematically made available in Russian, sometimes to such an extent that the original does not even get published any more, but only the translation.

What part does translated literature play in the migration of literary procedures from one polysystem to another? Think, for example, of the dominant position of the epic and the ode in French poetry from the Pléiade onwards, or of the "naturalization" of the sonnet into Chinese by Feng Chih. It often happens that a dominant meter is not, as could be expected, introduced into a literature by a "great" poet, but rather by a translator whose own work is relatively quickly forgotten. There is the case of Octavien de St. Gelais who introduced the alternation of masculine and feminine rhyme into French poetry through his translations of Ovid, or that of Johann Heinrich Voss whose Homer translations established the hexameter as the dominant meter for the classical period of German literature.

A further problem is that of the kinds of translating that have relatively little to do with the linguistic component of the work at all: the kind that "translates" works of literature from one social sphere to another (e.g., adult literature into children's literature), or the kind that is often responsible for the dissemination of the "image" of a work in a given culture by means of plot summaries in textbooks, condensed versions, etc.,[4] or the kind that puts literature into film or TV serials, or one genre into another. (It should be obvious, by the way, that some rewriting of literary history will become necessary as the result of this type of investigation.)

The scholar-translator's work, on the other hand, is of enormous heuristic value, especially if he or she translates from what a basically Eurocentric attitude persists in calling "exotic" literatures. This helps to establish and widen the canon of world literature—on condition that he or she translates into English or Russian.

In conclusion, we can say that the polysystem hypothesis, by focusing on the product rather than the process of translation, opens the way for the integration of translation theory into a theory of literature. It has "excess content" over its rivals in that it can account for phenomena which those rivals are, for the most part, unable to explain, such as pseudo-translations and the "sudden" appearance of literary procedures in a given polysystem (e.g. the Bildungsroman in German literature, which came out of translations, sponsored by Jesuits and exhibiting a moralising tendency, of the picaresque novel). Finally, the polysystem hypothesis may help integrate theory and practice: a knowledge of the way in which literary polysystems evolve may be conducive to attempts to actively influence that evolution as well as to describe it.

NOTES

1. Principal texts of the group include Itamar Even Zohar, *Papers in Historical Poetics* (Tel Aviv: The Porter Institute of Poetics and Semiotics, 1978); Lefevere, *Literary Knowledge* (Assen, the Netherlands; Van Gorcum, 1977); J. S. Holmes, José Lambert, and Raymond van den Broeck, eds., *Literature and Translation* (Louvain: Acco, 1978); Gideon Toury, *Norms of Literary Translation into Hebrew* (Tel Aviv: The Porter Institute of Poetics and Semiotics, forthcoming); Lefevere and van den Broeck, *Uitnodiging tot de Vertaalwetenschap* (Amsterdam; Coutinho, 1979); Lefevere and Lambert, *Littérature comparée, traduction littéraire, théorie de la littérature* (Paris: Minard, 1979); *Proceedings of the Colloquium on Translation and Intercultural Communication (Porter Institute, Tel Aviv, Summer 1978)*.

2. *Pavel Medvedev, Die formale Methode in der Literaturwissenschaft*, trans. Helmut Glueck (Stuttgart: Metzler, 1976).

3. Andreas Huyssen, *Die fruhromantische Konzeption von Uebersetzung und Aneigung* (Zurich: Atlantis Verlag, 1969), p. 120.

4. *Cf.* the work done by the Nitra Pedagogical Faculty, Czechoslovakia, by Anton Popovič and Imre Deneš.

Translation Sources in the Humanities and the Social Sciences

by Michael Jasenas

There are few other kinds of scholarly projects where successful undertaking is so dependent upon consulting appropriate bibliographic sources as is a translation project. The problems of a bibliographic nature encountered by translators frequently have seemed to be like those of checkmate. Indeed, after examining a considerable number of translation checklists, many translators embark on ambitious projects only to discover that the works they chose have already been translated. To prevent such a frustrating situation from occurring, bibliographic control of translations is of utmost importance.

The third quarter of this century saw a tremendous improvement in the bibliographic control of translations in the United States. The best control is understandably in the sciences and technology, because major support is usually given to bibliographic projects which bring the best returns. It is not surprising, therefore, to see that current translations in the sciences are quite well controlled by the present bibliographic services. The first such service of major importance was undertaken by the Special Libraries Association in 1953; after a period of two years it was updated and took the form of the *Translation Monthly* (1955-58) which has been continued from 1959 as *Technical Translations* and *The Translations Register-Index*. This service records the new accessions of the Special Libraries Association Translation Center as well as references to translations available from the Clearinghouse for Federal Scientific and Technical Information and from various commercial sources. The translations recorded by the Special Libraries Association Translation Center were consolidated in 1969 when the National Translation Center issued the *Consolidated*

Index of Translations into English, which is kept up to date by *The Translations Register-Index*. Although devoted to information about translations in the sciences and technology, these indexing services provide some coverage in the social sciences.

While business and industry provide the main support for translations in the fields of science and technology, the government supports considerably the translations of works dealing with the social sciences, especially international affairs, strategic planning, and economics. Of particular importance here is the United States Joint Publications Research Service (JPRS), established in 1957. It is an interagency organization which serves the foreign language needs of the federal government research organizations, providing translations of unclassified foreign documents, scholarly works, research reports, and other selected source materials. This agency is the largest producer of English-language translations, publishing annually over a quarter of a million pages of mimeographed translation manuscripts. This includes practically all fields in the social sciences and some scientific and technical fields. By providing adequate indexes for bibliographic control of its publications, the JPRS is of primary importance for social scientists in general and contemporary historians in particular.

The JPRS translations are indexed in the *Bibliography-Index to Current U.S. Joint Publications Research Service Translations*, 1962-1970, and the *Bibliography and Index to the United States Joint Publications Research Service (JPRS) Translations*, 1970/71-1973/74, which are continued by *Transdex* from 1974 onward. Another useful index of translations in the social sciences is the *Government Reports Announcements and Index* which records translations made in research supported by federal grants and contracts. There is also a series of bibliographies which, being primarily concerned with science and technology, nevertheless devote some attention to the listing of translations in the social sciences. Such bibliographies are: *World Index of Scientific Translations* (1967-71), *List of Translations Notified to ETC (European Translations Centre)*, and their successor *World Index of Scientific Translations Notified to the International Translations Centre* (1972-1977), which merged with *Translation Bulletin* and *Bulletin des Traducteurs* to form *World Transindex*.

Useful tools for locating translations in the social sciences are various bibliographies and guides to reading materials in English, such

MICHAEL JASENAS

as Nai-ruenn Chen's *Economy of Mainland China, 1949-1963: A Bibliography of Materials in English* (1963) and Robert A. Humphreys' *Latin American History: A Guide to the Literature in English* (1958).

For translated materials representing foreign newspaper coverage, foreign periodical articles, and foreign documents, for which no comprehensive bibliographic control has been established, translators may have to consult a variety of books and serials which publish documents and other source materials in English translation. Such publications in book form are, for example, Jane T. Degras' *Soviet Documents on Foreign Policy* (1951-53) and John C. Lane's *Source Materials on the Government and Politics of Germany* (1964). Serial publications of this type include: (1) for Germany: *The German Tribune: A Weekly Review of the German Press* (1962-); (2) for the Soviet Union: *Current Digest of the Soviet Press* (1949-), *Reprints from the Soviet Press* (1965-), *Samizdat Bulletin* (1973-), *Soviet Anthropology and Archaeology* (1962-), *Soviet Educaton* (1958-), *Soviet Geography: Review and Translations* (1968-), *Soviet Law and Government* (1962-), *Soviet Review: A Journal of Translations* (1960- *Soviet Sociology* (1962-), *Soviet Statutes and Decisions* (1964-), and *Soviet Studies in History* (1962-); and (3) for China: *Chinese Economic Studies* (1967-), *Chinese Law and Government* (1968-), *Chinese Sociology and Anthropology* (1968-), and *Chinese Studies in History* (1967-). Moreover, international covrage of this type of translations is supplemented by the *Daily Report, Foreign Radio Broadcast* which has been issued by the United States Foreign Broadcast Information Service five times per week since 1945 to furnish English translations of current news and commentary from foreign broadcasts, news agency transmissions, newspapers and periodicals relating to Western Europe, Soviet Union, Eastern Europe, Sub-Saharan Africa, Middle East and North Africa, Latin America, People's Republic of China, and Asia and the Pacific region.

Appended to the present article is a list recording the major bibliographic aids for locating translations in the humanities and in the social sciences. To supplement this list, translators should consult Eugene P. Sheehy's *Guide to Reference Books* which provides information on various bibliographies containing additional translation sources. There is, moreover, a British equivalent of Sheehy's guide, A. J. Walford's *Guide to Reference Material,* which also records translation sources not necessarily overlapping. Besides providing information on a number of translation bibliographies, these two guides record some valuable "hidden" sources of translations under the headings of various special fields.

The first section of the "Checklist of Major Sources for Translations into English" (below) records two major general bibliographies of translations. The first one, *Index translationum*, had covered twelve countries before it was interrupted by World War II. Presently published annually by UNESCO, it now covers over sixty countries. It is arranged by country, under which entries are listed according to the ten major headings of the Universal Decimal Classification (UDC). Within each of these ten areas titles are listed alphabetically by authors. The *Index translationum*, furthermore, contains indexes of authors, publishers, and translators. However, it is helpful to note that the headings of this source are in French and arranged alphabetically accordingly; therefore, one should look under "Etats-Unis" for United States at the beginning of the volume and under "Royaume-Uni" for Great Britain toward the end of the volume.

The two main shortcomings of *Index translationum* are: (1) a considerable time lag, usually four years, between the date of publication of a translation and its listing in the *Index translationum* (e.g., the *Index translationum* volume for translations published in 1974 was issued in 1978); and (2) lack of multiyear cumulations. This latter shortcoming was remedied in part by the publication of *Index translationum: Cumulative Index to English Translations, 1948-1968*, recording translations made in seven English-speaking countries (Australia, Canada, New Zealand, Ireland, Republic of South Africa, United Kingdom, and the United States). To overcome the first of the two shortcomings of the *Index translationum*, there exists a monthly card service, cumulated annually in book form, issued in Frankfurt am Main by Bentz since 1954, entitled *Chartotheca translationum alphabetica: Internationale Bibliographie der Übersetzungen*. It must be noted, moreover, that *Index translationum* lists only books (i.e., separately published translations), thus excluding translations which appear in periodicals or in collections of essays, poems or stories.

The second major bibliography indicated on the checklist below, under "I, A: General Bibliographies of Translations," *Literatures of the World in English Translation*, represents an attempt toward comprehensiveness in listing the works of literature of all the nations of the world. This ambitious bibliographic project was initiated in the 1940s by two national organizations, the National Council of Teachers of English and the American Library Association. Volume One of this bibliography, published in 1968, covers Greek, Latin, and Medieval literatures. Volume Two, published in the preceding year, covers Slavic literatures and is one of the best ever conceived for Slavic literatures in English translation. Volume Three of the *Literatures of the World*, published in 1970, consists of two parts: the first includes Catalan, Italian, Portuguese, Brazilian, Rumanian, Spanish, and Spanish-American literatures; the second covers French literature. Volume four, currently being prepared for publication, will cover Celtic, Germanic, and other European literatures. A fifth volume, also being planned, will deal with the literatures of Asia and Africa. In addition to the translations of literary works, the editors of this series of volumes have intended to list translations of important works of philosophy, history, science, and theology. The editors limit their scope, however, to the inclusion of more recent translations and those of reasonable length.

Included in the first section of the checklist below is the "List of Translations" covering English translations published since 1960. This list appears annually in the *Yearbook of Comparative and General Literature* since 1961. Although primarily concerned with listing translations of belles-lettres, the list also records a number of translations of critical works in the fields of general and comparative literature.

Useful sources for translations published in journals are bibliographies listing periodicals which are translated cover to cover or which contain selected translated articles or abstracts of publications. Such bibliographies are Richard C. Gremling's *English Language Equivalent Editions of Foreign Language Serials* (2nd ed., 1966) and *Translations Journals*, issued in 1973 by the European Translations Centre (superseded by the "List of Periodicals Translated . . ." included in the *World Index of Scientific Translations and List of Translations Notified to the International Translations Centre*, 1972-77). Although the aim of these bibliographies is to record translations in scientific and technical fields, some data included relate to the humanities and the social sciences.

There are, moreover, a number of general bibliographies supplementing or updating the conventional translation sources previously mentioned or sources recorded in parts B and C of section I of the checklist appended. Such bibliographies, also listed below in sections II and III, are American and British national bibliographies and printed catalogs of great research libraries, as well as the *National Union Catalog* which records holdings of American libraries.

For locating translations that are not published separately, further bibliographic sources, listed under "Indexes" in the checklist appended herewith, deal with particular literary genres, such as essays, plays, poems or short stories. One such source is the *Essay and General Literature Index*. By looking under the author's name in this index, one may find listed various essays which have been translated into English and published in a collection of essays but not separately.

Once all the categories of the bibliographic tools mentioned above have been exhausted, translators can find additional information by examining various author bibliographies. The latter may serve as adequate translation sources, provided they are up to date. There are certain types of author bibliographies whose titles usually indicate that they are most likely to contain translations of an author's works, for example, Armin Arnold's *Heine in England and America* (1959), *Schiller in England* (published by the Institute of Germanic Languages and Literatures in 1961), and *Khudozhestvennaia proizvedeniia L.N. Tolstogo v perevodakh na inostrannye iazyki* (published by Vsesoiuznaia Gosudarstvennaia Biblioteka Inostrannoi Literatury in 1961). In addition to separately published author bibliographies, there are large numbers which appear either as contributions to periodicals or as portions of books. A useful tool for locating such "hidden" bibliographies is the *Bibliographic Index*, a current bibliographic service in the United States. Special bibliographies listed in the *Bibliographic Index* may also be of some help to translators. Since some lists of an author's translated works are omitted from the *Bibliographic Index*, it is worthwhile to check certain works written about the author, which may include a list of the translations of the author's works. For example, in its bibliography section, Georges Lemaître's *Jean Giraudoux: The Writer and His Work* (1971) contains a list of "English Translations of Jean Giraudoux's Works," a list which the *Bibliographic Index* has failed to record. Sometimes the existence of such lists can be ascertained by checking a library's catalog cards. Although the *Bibliographic Index* intends to record separately published bibliographies as well, for the latter a useful tool is Theodore Besterman's *World Bibliography of Bibliographies* which provides information about bibliographies produced before 1937 and thus not recorded in the *Bibliographic Index*, the first cumulative volume of which was published in 1945.

In addition to the author bibliographies, some bibliographies covering a particular literary period, such as Robert Bossuat's *Manuel bibliographique de la littérature française du Moyen Age* (1951), provide information about translations of the works of that period. Furthermore, some general periodical indexes as well as those devoted to special fields (e.g., *MLA International Bibliography*) may provide information about translations not found in other sources. Many large research library special collections are also valuable to the translator. *Subject Collections: A Guide to Special Book Collections*, by Lee Ash, indicates libraries possessing important special collections. For example, the Theater Collection of the New York Public Library may help a translator find extensive information about foreign plays translated into English.

Checklist of Major Sources for Translations into English

I.   Bibliographies of Translations
     A.   General Bibliographies of Translations
          Chartotheca translationum alphabetica: Internationale bibliographie der Übersetzungen. 1954-. (Monthly card service).
          Index translationum. 1932-40, Nos. 1-31; n.s. v.1, 1948-. (Annual).
          "List of Translations," 1960-. *Yearbook of Comparative and General Literature*, nos. 10-, 1961-. (Annual).
          The Literatures of the World in English Translation: A Bibliography. Ed. George B. Parks and Ruth Z. Temple. 1967-.
     B.   Translation Sources in the Humanities
          (Subdivided by language and/or country. Devoted mostly to the humanities, some of these bibliographies do include translations in the fields of the social sciences as well.)
          1. Translations from Belorussian
             The Literatures of the World in English Translation, Vol. 2: *The Slavic Literatures.* 1967. (Covers Belorussian, Bulgarian, Croatian, Czech, Kashubian, Lusatian, Macedonian,

Polish, Russian, Serbian, Slovak, Slovenian, and Ukrainian literatures.)
2. Translations from Bulgarian, see #1 above.
3. Translations from Catalan
   The Literatures of the World in English Translation. Vol. 3, pt. 1., 1970.
4. Translations from Chinese
   Columbia University. Columbia College. *A Guide to Oriental Classics.* 2nd ed. 1975.
   Davidson, Martha. *A List of Published Translations from Chinese into English, French and German.* 1952-57.
   Gibbs, Donald A. *A Bibliography of Studies and Translations of Modern Chinese Literature, 1918-1942.* 1975.
5. Translations from Classical Languages and/or of Medieval Works
   Farrar, Clarissa P. *Bibliography of English Translations from Medieval Sources.* 1946.
   Ferguson, Marie Anne. *Bibliography of English Translations from Medieval Sources, 1943-1967.* 1974.
   Foster, F.M.K. *English Translations from the Greek.* 1918.
   The Literatures of the World in English Translation. Vol 1: *The Greek and Latin Literatures.* 1968.
   Smith, Frank S. *The Classics in Translation: an Annotated Guide to the Best Translations of the Greek and Latin Classics into English.* 1930; rpt. 1968.
6. Translations from Croatian, see #1 above.
7. Translations from Czech, see #1 above.
8. Translations from Danish
   Bredsdorff, Elias. *Danish Literature in English Translation.* 1950.
9. Translations from French
   The Literatures of the World in English Translation. Vol. 3, pt. 2. 1970.
10. Translations from German
    Bibliographie der Übersetzungen deutschsprachiger Werke. 1954-. (Quarterly).
    Mönnig, R., ed. *Translations from the German: English, 1948-1964.* 2nd rev. ed. 1969.
    Morgan, Bayard Q. *A Critical Bibliography of German Literature in English Translation, 1481-1927.* 2nd. ed. 1965. *Supplement Embracing the Years 1928-1955.* 1965.
    Smith, Murray F. *A Selected Bibliography of German Literature in English Translation, 1956-1960.* 1972.
11. Translations from Hebrew

Goell, Yohai. *Bibliography of Modern Hebrew Literature in English Translation.* 1968.
12. Translations from the Languages of India
   Columbia University. Columbia College. *A Guide to Oriental Classics.* 2nd ed. 1975.
   Emeneau, Murray B. *A Union List of Printed Indic Texts and Translations in American Libraries.* 1935.
   Jain, Sushil K. *A Bibliography of Indian Poetry in English.* 1967.
   Spencer, Dorothy M. *Indian Fiction in English: An Annotated Bibliography.* 1960.
13. Translations from Italian
   The Literatures of the World in English Translation. Vol. 3, pt. 1. 1970.
   Shields, Nancy C. *Italian Translations in America.* 1931.
14. Translations from Japanese
   Columbia University. Columbia College. *A Guide to Oriental Classics.* 2nd ed. 1975.
   P.E.N. Club, Japan. *Japanese Literature in European Languages.* 1961.
15. Translations from Kashubian, see #1 above.
16. Translations of Latin American Works
   Freudenthal, Juan R. *Index to Anthologies of Latin American Literature in English Translation.* 1977.
   Hulet, Claude L. *Latin American Poetry in English Translation: A Bibliography.* 1965. . *Latin American Prose in English Translation: A Bibliography.* 1964.
   Leavitt, Sturgis E. *Hispano-American Literature in the United States: A Bibliography of Translations and Criticism.* 2 vols. 1932-35.
   Levine, Suzanne J. *Latin America: Fiction and Poetry in Translation.* 1970.
   The Literatures of the World in English Translation. Vol. 3, pt. 1. 1970.
   Shaw, Bradley A. *Latin American Literature in English Translation: An Annotated Bibliography.* 1976.
17. Translations from Lusatian, see #1 above.
18. Translations from Macedonian, see # 1 above.
19. Translations of Philippine Works
   Yapes, L.Y. *Philippine Literature in English, 1898-1957.* 1958.
20. Translations of Oriental Works
   Columbia University. Columbia College. *A Guide to Oriental Classics.* 2nd ed. 1975.

21. Translations from Polish
   Coleman, Marion M. *Polish Literature in English Translation.* 1963.
   Hoskins, J.W. *Polish Books in English, 1945-1971.* 1974.
   Maciuszko, J.J. *The Polish Short Story in English: A Guide and Critical Bibliography.* 1968.
   Taborski, B. *Polish Plays in English Translation.* 1968.
   See also #1 above.
22. Translations from Portuguese
   The Literatures of the World in English Translation. Vol. 3, pt. 1. 1970.
23. Translations from Provençal, see #22 above.
24. Translations from Rumanian, see #22 above.
25. Translations from Russian
   Bibliography of Russian Literature in English Translation to 1945. 1972. (Consists of M.B. Line's *A Bibliography of Russian Literature in English Translation to 1900* and A. Ettlinger and J.M. Gladstone's *Russian Literature, Theatre and Art ... 1900-1945.*)
   Gibian, George. *Soviet Russian Literature in English.* 1967.
   Proizvedeniia sovetskikh pisatelei v perevodakh na inostrannye iazyki... 1945-. 1954-.
   See also #1 above.
26. Translations from Serbian, see # 1 above.
27. Translations from Slovak, see #1 above.
28. Translations from Slovenian, see #1 above.
29. Translations from Spanish
   The Literatures of the World in English Translation. Vol. 3, pt. 1. 1970.
   Pane, Remigio U. *English Translations from the Spanish, 1484-1943.* 1944.
   Rudder,R.S. *The Literature of Spain in English Translation.* 1975.
30. Translations from Ukrainian, see #1 above.

C. Translation Sources in the Social Sciences
   1. Bibliographies and Indexes Devoted Primarily to the Social Sciences
   Bibliography-Index to Current U.S. Joint Publications Research Service Translations. July/Sept. 1962-June 1970.
   Bibliography and Index to the United States Joint Publications Research Service (JPRS) Translations. 1970/71-1973/74.
   Government Reports Announcements. 1946-.
   Government Reports Announcements and Index, 1975-.

Government Reports Index, 1965-.

Transdex, 1974-.

White, Thomas N. *Guide to United States J.P.R.S. Research Translations, 1957-1966.* 1966.

2. Bibliographies and Indexes Devoted to Scientific Translations but Including Limited Social Science Coverage

European Translations Centre. *List of Translations Notified to ETC.* Vols. 1-6. 1967-71.

National Translations Center. *Consolidated Index of Translations into English.* 1969.

Special Libraries Association Translations Center. *Translations Register-Index.* 1972-. (Updates the *Consolidated Index of Translations into English.*)

World Index of Scientific Translations. 1967-71.

World Index of Scientific Translations and List of Translations Notified to the International Translations Centre. 1972-77.

World Transindex. 1977-.

II. National Bibliographies
  A. American
    1. Early

    Church, Elihu D. *Catalogue of Books Relating to the Discovery and Early History of North and South America, Forming Part of the Library of E.D. Church.* Comp. and annotated by George Watson Cole. 5 vols. 1907.

    Sabin, Joseph. *Dictionary of Books Relating to America.* 29 vols. 1868-1936.

    Shipton, C.K., and J.E. Mooney. *National Index to American Imprints through 1801: The Short-Title Evans.* 2 vols. 1969.

    Thompson, L.S. *The New-Sabin.* 1974-.

    2. Nineteenth Century

    Shaw, R.R., and R.H. Shoemaker. *American Bibliography: Preliminary Checklist.* 22 vols. 1958-66.

    Roorbach, O.A. *Bibliotheca Americana, 1820-61.* 2 vols. 1852-61.

    Kelly, James. *American Catalogue of Books Published in the United States from Jan. 1861 to Jan. 1871.* 2 vols. 1866-71.

    American Catalogue of Books, 1876-1910. 9 vols. in 13. 1876-1910; rpt. 1941.

    3. Twentieth Century

    United States Catalog: Books in Print, 1899-Jan. 1, 1923. 1900-28.

4. Current

American Book Publishing Record. 1960-. (Monthly, with annual and five-year cumulations).

Books in Print. 1948-. (Annual).

Cumulative Book Index, 1928/32-. (Monthly, except August, with semi-annual, annual and multiyear cumulations).

Paperbound Books in Print. 1955-. (Monthly).

Publishers' Trade List Annual. 1873—.

Publishers' Weekly. 1872-. (Cumulated monthly to form *American Book Publishing Record*).

B. British

1. General

Lowndes, W.T. *Bibliographer's Manual of English Literature.* 6 vols in 11. 1858-64.

2. Early

Pollard, A.W., and G. R. Redgrave. *Short-Title Catalogue of Books Printed in England, Scotland, and Ireland and of English Books Printed Abroad, 1475-1640.* 1926.

Bishop, W.W. *A Checklist of American Copies of "Short-Title Catalogue" Books.* 1950.

Edmonds, C.K. "Huntington Library Supplement to the Record of its Books in the Short-Title Catalogue." *Huntington Library Bulletin*, No. 4 (1933), 1-152.

Wing, D.G. *Short-Title Catalogue of Books Printed in England, Scotland, Ireland, and British America and of English Books Printed in Other Countries, 1641-1700.* 3 vols. 1945-51.

3. Nineteenth and Twentieth Centuries

British Books in Print. 1967-. (Annual).

British National Bibliography. 1950-. (Weekly, with four-month cumulations and annual volume).

English Catalogue of Books, 1801-1968. 1969.

Whitaker's Cumulative Book List: A Classified List of Publications. 1924-. (Quarterly, cumulating annually).

III. Library Catalogs

British Museum. Department of Printed Books. *General Catalogue of Printed Books.* Photolithographic ed. to 1955. 263 vols. 1965-66.

.. *Ten-Year Supplement, 1956-1965.* 50 vols. 1968.

.. *Five-Year Supplement, 1966-1970.* 26 vols. 1971-72.

California University. University at Los Angeles. *Dictionary Catalog of the University Library, 1919-1962.* 129 vols. 1963.

Deutscher Gesamtkatalog. Bd. 1-14. 1931-39. (Supple-

mented by its *Neue Titel*, 1893- 1944, and *Berliner Titeldrucke*, 1930/34-35/39).
The National Union Catalog: Pre-1956 Imprints. 1968-.
Paris. Bibliothèque Nationale. *Catalogue général des livres imprimés: Auteurs.* 1900-.
.. *Catalogue général des livres imprimés: auteurs, collectivités-auteurs, anonymes, 1960-1969.* Série 1: Caractères latins. 23 vols. 1972-76.
U.S. Library of Congress. *A Catalog of Books Represented by the Library of Congress Printed Cards, Issued to July 31, 1942.* 167 vols. 1942-46.
.. *Supplement, 1942-1962.* 152 vols. 1969-71.
.. *1963-1967.* 59 vols. 1969.
.. *1968-1972.* 104 vols. 1973.
.. *1973-1977.* 135 vols. 1978.
.. *1978-.* (Annual cumulations).
.. *Library of Congress Catalog, Books: Subjects, 1950-1954. 20 vols. 1955.*
.. *1955-1959.* 22 vols. 1960.
.. *1960-1964.* 25 vols. 1965.
.. *1965-1969. 42 vols. 1970.*
.. *1970-. (Annual cumulations).*

IV. Indexes
  A. Essays

      Essay and General Literature Index, 1900-1933. 1934.
      .. *1934-1940.* 1941
      .. *1941-1947.* 1948.
      .. *1948-1954.* 1955.
      .. *1955-1959.* 1960
      .. *1960-1964.* 1965.
      .. *1965-1969.* 1970.
      .. *1970-1974.* 1975.
      (Kept up to date by semiannual, annual, and final five-year cumulations).

  B. Fiction

      Baker, E.A., and James Packman. *Guide to the Best Fiction.* 1932.
      Chicorel Index to Short Stories in Anthologies and Collections. 4 vols. 1974.
      Cole, W.R. *A Checklist of Science Fiction Anthologies.* 1964.
      Contento, William. *Index to Science Fiction Anthologies and Collections.* 1978.
      Hannigan, F.J. *Standard Index of Short Stories, 1900-1914.* 1918.

Index to the Science-Fiction Magazines, 1926-1950. Comp. by D.B. Day. 1952.

Index of Science Fiction Magazines, 1951-1965. Comp. by Norm Metcalf. 1968.

Index to the Science Fiction Magazines, 1962-1967. New England Science Fiction Association, 1971.

Index to the Weird Fiction Magazines, 1962-1967. New England Science Fiction Association, 1971.

The MIT's Science Fiction Society's Index to the S-F Magazines, 1951-1965. Comp. by Erwin S. Strauss. 1966.

Short Story Index: An Index to 60,000 Stories in 4320 Collections. Comp. by D.E. Cook and I.S. Monro. 1953.

.. Supplements, 1950-. 1956-.

Siemon, Frederick. *Science Fiction Story Index, 1950-1968.* 1971.

C. Drama

Chicorel Theater Index to Plays. 5 vols. 1970-74.

Firkins, I.T.E. *Index to Plays, 1800-1926.* 1927.

Ireland, N.O. *Index to Full Length Plays 1944 to 1964.* 1965.

Keller, D.H. *Index to Plays in Periodicals.* 1971.

Logasa, H., and W. Ver Noy. *An Index to One- Act Plays.* 1942.

.. Supplements 1-5, 1924-64. 1932-66.

Ottemiller, J.H. *Index to Plays in Collections ... Published between 1900 and early 1976.* 1976.

Patterson, Charlotte A. *Plays in Periodicals.* 1970.

Play Index, 1949-52, 1953-60, 1961-67, 1968-72, 1973-77, 5 vols. 1953-78.

Thomson, Ruth G. *Index to Full Length Plays, 1895 to 1925.* 1956.

.. *Index to Full Length Plays, 1926 to 1944.* 1946.

D. Poetry

Chicorel Index to Poetry in Anthologies and Collections in Print. 4 vols. 1974.

Chicorel Index to Poetry in Anthologies and Collections: Retrospective. 4 vols. 1975.

Granger's Index to Poetry. 6th ed. ... Indexing Anthologies Published through December 31, 1970. 1973.

Granger's Index to Poetry, 1970-1977. 1978.

Maximizing Computer Assistance in Literary Translation: Petrarch's *Familiares*

by Aldo S. Bernardo

Anyone familiar with computer technology could not be too surprised by retrenchments and cutbacks that have recently struck particularly hard at the use of such technology in the humanities. Most computer centers have had to limit technical support either to administrative usage or to projects that have been handsomely funded by outside granting agencies. For these reasons, I felt it appropriate to avail myself of such technology very early to see if it might assist in a project that had ramifications far beyond those immediately obvious.

Having devoted most of my scholarly life to the Italian Humanist, Francis Petrarch, I turned my attention to the possibility of having the computer assist me in the translation of his Latin prose works, particularly his correspondence. Such assistance, however, was meant not only to expedite the process of translation itself, but to provide a variety of additional possibilities that went beyond mere translation ... especially considering that Petrarch's Latin had served as a model for the early and high Renaissance.

A casual conversation held with the director of the SUNY-Binghamton computer center convinced me that there was a variety of ways in which the computer could assist me. The one that seemed to have the greatest potential was the preparation of a Latin-English in-context word list of Petrarch's correspondence that would start with the first word of the first letter and end with the last word of the last letter. This would result in a veritable Latin-English dictionary of Petrarch's Latin, but arranged in a manner that would allow me to dictate the English translation into a dictaphone directly from the computer printout. Perhaps even more important was the fact that, through careful planning, the dictionary prepared for the most significant collection of earlier letters known as the *Familiares* could simplify still further the translation of the other prose works, since the number of new words or forms could not exceed by very much the better than 280,000 forms that comprised the 350 letters of the collection. As a result, the English meanings for each word or form of subsequent collections would be restricted to the one or two used most frequently for the same word or form in the *Familiares*, each of whose forms had been assigned up to six meanings. In brief, the in-context word list for the second translation would itself essentially be a non-idiomatic translation of the text. While the non-idiomatic nature of such a translation may at times reach extremes, a basic knowledge of Latin would ordinarily suffice to unscramble the words in order to attain meaning. For example, the first sentences of the *Familiari* would first emerge from the computer as they do in Figure 1:

> *To Socrates his.*
> What indeed now do, brother? Behold, already almost everything try, and nowhere rest. When it expect?

A knowledge of Latin syntax and verb endings readily clarifies the meaning for the first draft:

> *To his Socrates.*
> What indeed are we to do now, brother? Alas, we have already tried almost everything, and nowhere is there rest. When are we to expect it?

The assistance of the computer would thus become cumulative with each new work or text. Even more exciting is the possibility of programming in such a way that the dictionary for the second work could easily be integrated with the one for the first work, as could any subsequent ones. The ramifications of such flexibility could eventually lead to the generation of a Humanistic and Renaissance Latin-English dictionary through the simple process of integrating into the basic Petrarchan dictionary words and forms of significant Latin words written through the early Renaissance, say through Bembo and his school. This would result in a Dictionary of Humanistic and Renaissance Latin that would have its roots solidly based in the home soil of Petrarch's Latin style. Two grants, one rather substantial, from the SUNY Research Foundation enabled the project to get off to a good start.

The translation project included the following phases:

1. Keypunch and verify the entire text of the four volumes of the Vittorio Rossi edition of the *Familiares*, the monumental definitive edition completed by Umberto Bosco (Firenze, 1933-42). It was decided to retain the pagination and paragraphing of this edition in order to provide a ready location reference for each word form.(see Figure 2).

2. Using the keypunched cards, create a magnetic tape record for each word in the text, its location in the volumes, and a serially assigned identification number. This became the location file.

3. Generate an alphabetical listing of all the words, indicating the number of times the word appears and the location for each of its appearances (see Figure 3).

4. Generate a translation list (Figure 4) consisting of all word forms in alphabetical sequence and having the following parameters: up to six English equivalents and up to 15 characters for each English equivalent. (This step was accomplished with the assistance of 5 Latinists who spent an entire summer making entries on special printout sheets).

5. Generate a concordance showing each word in context, its location in the Rossi text according to volume, book, page, and line, and the number of its occurrences (see Figure 5). (This proved to be the unexpected bonus that could eventually contribute significantly to the Dictionary.)

6. Create an in-context printout of the Latin words with corresponding English translations. The output would have Latin words along the left margin and English translations immediately following (see Figure 1).

7. Using the in-context printout, the investigator can dictate idiomatic translation into a dictating unit, selecting the most likely word translations as provided in the example below (see Figure 6.)

The entire project required approximately 75 hours of computer time. If done manually, such a project would have required an estimated 10 years.

This approach thus made maximum use of the assistance of computer technology by exploiting to the fullest its "memory bank" capacity. By preparing not only carefully numbered and alphabetized lists of original Latin forms, but also a corresponding list of English meanings, the approach provided the potential for a concordance and for a Latin-English dictionary. By then programming both lists to produce a master list containing an in-context printout of the Latin words with corresponding English meanings, the translation process was immeasurably simplified. The further potential of integrating fifteenth and sixteenth-century humanistic texts into these lists should eventually provide an historical perspective of changing Latin forms and meanings from Petrarch through the early Renaissance. Thus, instead of a project having a single goal, we had one with a variety of significant potentials.

The translation of the *Familiari* is approaching the two-thirds mark with the completion of Book VI. The first volume containing the first eight books has already appeared in *Rerum familiarium libri I-VIII*, trans. Aldo S. Bernardo (Albany: SUNY Press, 1955). About three quarters of the 1501 edition of the *Senili* has already been keypunched and a preliminary printout prepared. A small grant for this project has been secured from NEH. Unlike the first project, this one will entail the publication of the Latin text which presently exists in printed form in sixteenth-century editions.

With the restricted availability of the computer to humanistic scholars, it has become necessary for such scholars to enlarge the scope of their research in order to gain support of a technology that appears to become more expensive with each passing day. The secret lies in working with top-flight programmer analysts capable of generating a data bank that can provide the scholar with a variety of kinds of information rather than a single kind. There is little question that grant availability will increase significantly if this is done.

ALDO S. BERNARDO

```
SUNY/BINGHAMTON TEXT PROCESSOR -- PETRARCH TRANSLATION LISTING        V.B.L.PAGELN    WORD NO.
   AD              TO/AT/UNTIL/TOWARDS/FOR                            010101000301    00000001
   SOCRATEM        SOCRATES                                          010101000301    00000002
   SUUM.           HIS/HER/ITS/THEIR/PROPER/SUITABLE/FAVOURABLE      010101000301    00000003
 * QUID            WHO/WHAT/ANYBODY/ANYTHING/ANYONE                   010101000302    00000004
   VERO            IN TRUTH/REALLY/INDEED/IN FACT/CERTAINLY           010101000302    00000005
   NUNC            NOW/AT PRESENT/AT THIS MOMENT/ALREADY/NOW...NOW    010101000302    00000006
   AGIMUS,         DO/ACT/DRIVE/WORK/SPEND/THANK/BEHAVE/UNDERTAKE/DIRECT/  010101000302  00000007
   FRATER?         BROTHER                                           010101000302    00000008
   ECCE,           BEHOLD/LOOK                                       010101000302    00000009
   IAM             NOW/ALREADY                                       010101000302    00000010
   FERE            ALMOST/ABOUT                                      010101000302    00000011
   OMNIA           ALL/EVERY/WHOLE/EVERYTHING                        010101000302    00000012
   TENTAVIMUS,     PROVE/TRY/TEST/ATTEMPT                            010101000302    00000013
 S ET             AND/ALSO                                           010101000303    00000014
   NUSQUAM         NOWHERE/IN NOTHING/ON NO OCCASION/TO,FOR NOTHING  010101000303    00000015
   REQUIES,        REST/REPOSE                                       010101000303    00000016
   ILLAM           WHEN/EVERY/AT THE TIME WHEN/SINCE BECAUSE         010101000303    00000017
   ILLAM           THAT/HER/IT                                       010101000303    00000018
 S EXPECTAMUS?     WAIT FOR/EXPECT/HOPE FOR                          010101000303    00000019
 S UBI            WHERE/WHEN/AS SOON AS/WHEREBY/WITH WHOM            010101000304    00000020
```

Figure 1. Latin / English translation listing

```
xxxxx PETRARCH TRANSLATION PROJECT -- PROOFREADERS LISTING

VOLUME 1  BOOK 01  LETTER 01  PAGE 0003

01      AD SOCRATEM SUUM.                                                     00002
02      QUID VERO NUNC AGIMUS, FRATER? ECCE, IAM FERE OMNIA TENTAVIMUS,       00003
03   ET NUSQUAM REQUIES; QUANDO ILLAM EXPECTAMUS?                             00003
04   UBI EAM QUERIMUS? TEMPORA, UT AIUNT, INTER DIGITOS EFFLUXERUNT;          00004
05   SPES NOSTRE VETERES CUM AMICIS SEPULTE SUNT. MILLESIMUS                  00005
06   TRECENTESIMUS QUADRAGESIMUS OCTAVUS ANNUS EST, QUI NOS SOLOS             00006
07   ATQUE INOPES FECIT; NEQUE ENIM EA NOBIS ABSTULIT, QUE INDO               00006
08   AUT CASPIO CARPATHIO VE MARI RESTAURARI QUEANT IRREPARABILES             00007
09   SUNT ULTIME IACTURE: ET QUODCUNQUE MORS INTULIT, IMMEDICABILE            00008
10   VULNUS EST. UNUM EST SOLAMEN SEQUEMUR ET IPSI QUOS                       00009
11   PREMISIMUS. QUE QUIDEM EXPECTATIO QUAM BREVIS FUTURA SIT,                00010
12   NESCIO; HOC SCIO, QUOD LONGA ESSE NON POTEST. QUANTULACUNQUE             00010
13   SANE EST, NON POTEST ESSE NON MOLESTA. SED A QUERELIS                    00011
14   SALTEM IN PRINCIPIO TEMPERANDUM EST. TIBI, FRATER, QUENAM                00012
15   TUI CURA SIT, QUID DE TE IPSO COGITES, IGNORO; EGO IAM SARCINULAS        00013
16   COMPONO, ET QUOD MIGRATURI SOLENT, QUID MECUM DEFERAM,                   00014
17   QUID INTER AMICOS PARTIAR, QUID IGNIBUS MANDEM, CIRCUMSPICIO.            00014
18   NICHIL ENIM VENALE MICHI EST. SUM SANE DITIOR SEU, VERIUS,               00015
19   IMPEDITIOR QUAM PUTABAM MULTA MICHI SCRIPTORUM DIVERSI                    00016
20   GENERIS SUPELLEX DOMI EST, SPARSA QUIDEM ET NEGLECTA.                     00017
21   PERQUISIVI SITU IAM SQUALENTES ARCULAS, ET SCRIPTURAS CARIE              00018
22   SEMESAS PULVERULENTUS EXPLICUI. IMPORTUNUS MICHI MUS NOCUIT              00018
23   ATQUE EDACISSIMUM TINEE VULGUS; ET PALLADIAS RES AGENTEM                 00019

xxxx END OF PAGE xxxx  WORDS THIS PAGE = 0190
```

Figure 2. Printout of text

```
FREQUENCY    WORD        *V BK LT PAGE LN *V BK LT PAGE LN *V BK LT PAGE LN *V BK LT PAGE LN *V BK LT PAGE LN
   1 ABBATIS         *2 11 01 0323 07
   1 ABDERE          *3 13 04 0063 23
   1 ABDEREM         *4 22 03 0110 01
   1 ABDI            *1 03 07 0118 08
   1 ABDICANDO       *4 20 13 0037 30
   1 ABDICASSET      *1 03 13 0133 07
   1 ABDICAVI        *4 22 17 0131 17
   1 ABDIDERAT       *2 05 07 0024 33
   1 ABDIDERIT       *3 16 09 0199 30
   1 ABDIDIT         *4 22 02 0105 29
   3 ABDITA          *1 03 01 0109 15 *2 09 13 0248 06 *1 16 06 0192 76
   1 ABDITAM         *1 04 01 0160 27
   1 ABDITARUMQUE    *1 03 01 0106 14
   1 ABDITAS         *1 04 12 0183 14 *2 10 05 0317 12
   1 ABDITE          *2 08 07 0178 11
   1 ABDITI          *2 11 12 0351 27
   4 ABDITIS         *1 01 09 0048 04 *2 07 03 0103 19 *3 15 09 0162 37 *4 24 10 0248 04
   1 ABDITO          *1 03 03 0112 14
   5 ABDITOS         *3 14 04 0104 02 *3 14 04 0115 09 *3 15 04 0161 18 *4 20 11 0034 19 *4 22 05 0115 01
   2 ABDITUM         *1 03 06 0116 05 *4 24 01 0214 17
   2 ABDITUS         *3 16 09 0197 31 *4 20 08 0031 32
   1 ABDUC           *1 02 07 0087 32
   1 ABDUCERE        *1 02 07 0086 26
```

Figure 3. Alphabetical word listing

78

```
PETRARCH BASIC DICTIONARY

A                1FROM/BY/AFTER/BECAUSE OF/
ABACTUM          1STEAL
ABBAS            1ABBOT
ABDERE           1OF ABDERA/OF ASPEROSA
ABDEREM          1WITHDRAW/HIDE
ABDI             1HIDE
ABDICANDO        1RENOUNCE/REJECT
ABDIDERAT        1WITHDRAW/HIDE/CONCEAL
ABDITA           1SECRET/CONCEALED/HIDDEN
ABDUC            1TAKE AWAY/BELIEVE/LEAD AWAY
ABEAM            1GO AWAY/RETIRE/DEPART/DISAPPEAR/VANISH/PASS AWAY/CHANGE
ABERRANTEM       1WANDER/LOSE ONE'S WAY/DEVIATE
ABES             1GO AWAY/RETIRE/DEPART/BE ABSENT/VANISH/PASS AWAY/CHANGE
ABHINC           1HEREAFTER/AGO
ABHORRENT        1SHRINK FROM/INCONSISTENT WITH/OPPOSED TO/INAPPROPRIATE
ABI              1GO AWAY/DEPART
ABICE            1THROW AWAY/STRIKE DOWN/LET GO/GIVE UP/ABANDON
ABIENS           1GO AWAY/DEPART
ABITU            1DEPARTURE
```

Figure 4. Translation list

```
PETRARCH CONCORDANCE --- SUNY BINGHAMTON

1 01 04 0025 01  EVERSAM CHORINTUM, POST VASTATAM ETHOLIAM, POST ARGOS AC MYCENAS CETEPASQUE URBES TRIUMPHATAS, POST MACEDONIE PECES
00001 MYCENAS
3 17 01 0226 27  IN EVANGELIO LEGIMUS, INGENTIS CUIUSDAM INEFFABILISQ E MYSTERII FUISSE, SIGNANTEM VELO VETERI, QUO USQUE IN ILLUD
00001 MYSTERII
2 10 01 0279 24  ERANT QUE GEREBAS, MAIORA TAMEN PUERILIS EXPEDITIONIS MYSTERIO VELABANTUR, NE SCILICET EAM PATRIAX VIR TIMERES,
2 10 04 0307 13  ALIQUID IMPORTANT. NAM ET INDE, HOC EST DEINDE, NON SINE MYSTERIO DICTUM EST, QUIA VIRGILIUM PUER IAM, IDEST NON IA
00002 MYSTERIO
3 17 01 0225 04    DEUS, PER VERBUM, QUIA BONA EST, UT CUM ALTITUDINE MYSTICA NOBIS IPSA TRINITAS INTIMETUR, HOC EST PATER ET
00001 MYSTICA
1 02 03 0068 35  AD CICERONEM BRUTUS REFERT VIDISSE SE EUM VIDELICET MYTILENIS EXULEM TAM INFRACTO ANIMO TAMQUE AVIDO BONORUM
00001 MYTILENIS
1 03 13 0131 19  "RUSTICUM" AIT ILLA, "ET HIRSUTUM HOSPITEM NACTA ERAM, QUI ME FAME AC LABORE PERPETUO CRUCIABAT, QUI
2 16 02 0058 35  QUOQUE DE EA PARTE PHILOSOPHIE QUE MORES INSTRUIT, HINC NACTA COGNOMEN INTERDUM VERO DE ARTIBUS ET DE
3 16 16 0046 18  MORUM CETERUM INTER MALOS INSTABILE FUNDAMENTUM NACTA, FAMILIARITAS EVI BREVIS EST; INGENS AUTEM BONIS
00003 NACTA
4 22 12 0131 01  EXTREMAMQUE THOPROBANEN HABITAREM HANC OCCASIONEM NACTI QUI DICUNTUR SERVI CUM SINT HOSTES ASPERRIMI, ET SUI
4 22 14 0152 13  CUM SUIS DUCIBUS DE VIRTUTE NUNQUAM SED SI SUI SIMILES NACTI SUNT, DE SOMNO ATQUE EBRIETATE CONTENDUNT, ET ILLORU
```

Figure 5. Concordance

ALDO S. BERNARDO

Francesco Petrarca, <u>Rerum familiarium libri</u>, trans. by A. S. Bernardo

---

Book I, 1

To his Socrates

What are we to do now, dear brother? Alas, we have already tried almost everything and no rest is in sight. When can we expect some? Where shall we seek it? Time, as they say, has slipped through our fingers; our former hopes are buried with our friends. The year of 1348 left us alone and helpless; it did not deprive us of things that can be restored by the Indian or Caspian or Carpathian Sea. It subjected us to irreparable losses. Whatever death wrought, is now an incurable wound.

There is only one consolation in all this: we too shall follow those who preceded us. How long our wait will be I do not know; but this I do know, that it cannot be long. And however short it may be, it cannot avoid being burdensome.

But we must desist from complaining, at least for now. I do not know what your preoccupations may be or what you may be thinking. As for me, I am arranging my belongings in little bundles, like migrants are wont to do. I am considering what to bring with me, what to share with friends, and what to burn. I have nothing to be put up for sale. Indeed I am richer or perhaps I should say more hampered than I thought, because of the great number of writings of different kinds that lie scattered and neglected throughout my house. I searched in squalid containers lying in hidden places and pulled out dusty writings half destroyed by decay. I was attacked by a frightened mouse and by a multitude of worms; and the spider of friendly Pallas attacked me for doing the work of Pallas. But there is nothing that unyielding and constant labor cannot overcome. Therefore, beset and encircled by confused heaps of letters and formless piles of paper, I began a first attack by determining to throw everything into the fire, thereby avoiding a thankless kind of labor.

Figure 6. Idiomatic translation

In Scholarly Pursuit

by Marcia Nita Doron

Scholarly translation is vertically boundless in its potential coverage of the world of knowledge. On a creative scale it lies between the literary and the technical. The former has been pursued and disputed for centuries. In the Hellenistic Era the Bible had already been translated from its original Hebrew into Greek[1]; the works of Homer were early translated and have since been rendered into a formidable array of languages.[2] The latter—technical translation—has been recognized as a major field in its own right for over a quarter of a century. Since World War II, scientific and technical works have been systematically translated and subject to bibliographic control.[3] While some attempt is being made to keep abreast of and encourage scholarly translation, major works in many fields and languages will remain unknown to academicians around the world. The reference here is not only to the predominantly quantitative areas of the social sciences, but psychology, sociology, political science, anthropology, history, philosophy and other disciplines as well.

We may all be familiar, at least summarily, with the works of Marx and Weber. But how often do we pause to realize that it is through the efforts of translators that these texts have become basic reading material in countless nations?[4] Giants such as Easton in political science, Toynbee in history, William James in psychology, Samuelson in economics, Meade in anthropology, Parsons in sociology and Dewey in philosophy have been translated into a plethora of languages.[5] In how many tongues, however, can students read William Riker's theory of coalitions or Marc Bloch's insights on medieval France? How many scholars around the world can benefit from Abraham Maslow's discussion of peak experiences or Milton Friedman's school of economic thought? In the fields of anthropology, sociology and philosophy, how many curricula will fail to include the works of Radcliffe Brown, Edwin Schur and John Rawls—all for the lack of systematic and quality translations?[6]

Translation in the social sciences bears its own inherent difficulties. First we should note that this type of translation is burdened with both the intricacies of literary translations and the technicalities of scientific translations. As in literary translation, the author/translator must follow Steiner's "hermeneutic motion."[7] The translator must know the author: his previous works, style, and background. Further, a deep understanding of and feeling for the text is essential: its rhythm, color, and design. All this pertains to scholarly translations, for these, too, were written by people with unique personalities, feelings and preferences—traits which we often illogically ascribe exclusively to creative writers. Moving on to the scientific, we find that in the social sciences, too, we must grapple with intraspecific terminology, with the question of translation or transliteration, with conversions of weights and measures. We must be careful not to alter meaning through a thoughtless turn of a phrase or a whimsical reorganization of sentence structure. Translation in the social sciences requires the flair of literary and the accuracy of scientific translations.

What are the special rigors of scholarly translation? What are some strategies to use in dealing with these? Every translator will work out his own system for "attacking" a text. This article presents a theoretical guide for approaching and pursuing an actual translation. We are not suggesting a static order. Each phase in our scenario will have to be accomplished, but each translator will surely find a personalized, optimal plan.

Translation Strategy

You have just received a text on land reallocation in eighteenth-century agrarian France. You may review the text and decide that the task is beyond your capabilities. You may, alternatively, decide to invest your efforts in the challenge. A reasonable beginning would be repeated readings of the material in question. You should have an idea of the breadth and scope of the subject. Find the major issues that are dealt with and begin your research. One point of departure might be the author's own bibliography. This will probably prove insufficient. You will need works in the field, originals and translations. This is perhaps the only way to deal with rendering those words, phrases, and concepts which have intraspecific meaning. If possible, get a specialist in the field to identify a good translator for you. You will need to determine the quality of the translations with which you are working. Look for anachronisms, awkward phraseology, inconsistencies. Is the translated text comprehensible, does it flow, are the terms comparable to those which are most commonly used in that area of concentration? The author himself may have acknowledged the capabilities of the translator. This may or may not be of import. In any case, the key is discrimination. You must begin to develop your own tools for discrimination between the over-general and the precise, the vague and the specific, the outdated and the up-to-date. Avail yourself of special dictionaries and glossaries. Be sure to mark specific references. You may need these later in footnotes, or for personal clarification. This information must be at your fingertips. Each term may carry a different meaning in varying contexts, time periods, regions, etc. Check and recheck these possible variations. Have available well-written English-language works in the field. The more you have read, the better you will be able to deal with nuances.

As you now begin the actual work of translation, you may find highly specific references, bordering on or outside the actual field of the work. These must be researched as well, although less extensively. Misinterpreting a single term might (or probably will) influence the veracity, quality and precision of your translation. The author may refer to an obscure individual or event which you have not encountered in your reading. To avoid still further research, you may prevail upon other resources. A living author can be approached for clarification. If you are in an academic community, you have the advantage of being able to call upon the expertise of individuals in other departments. Large libraries, of course, have reference departments, and professional associations may have resource persons at their headquarters. For example, it might be simpler and more expedient to write or call the American Bible Society than to search out a phrase in a text with which you may be unfamiliar.

Slowly, you translate. Studiously, you render terms and phrases into the target language.[8] Checking, always, your own consistency of terms and style, you complete the first draft of your work. Detail will now become more important: capitalization, tense, punctuation, syntax, structure. Cutting long, difficult sentences is legitimate, for example. However, in so doing you may have altered the author's style too dramatically. You may be dealing with what you consider to be a poorly written original. Certainly, some mending on your part, while remaining true to context, could only improve the translation. In this subfield of translation, adaptation to accepted American practices is expected.

Finally, impose yourself on an outside reader. Feedback, criticism, editorial comments—these are invaluable to a polished text, one which becomes a scholarly accomplishment in its own right, one which can stand alone in its field and meet any given academic standard and inspection.

Tactical Maneuvers

The scenario sketched above is certainly impressive, but perhaps it would be more helpful to delve into specifics. Let us return to our work on eighteenth-century agrarian France and the economic strategies and repercussions of land reallocations in this period. Intraspecific terminology abounds. Economic and dated terms must be dealt with. The term *produit*, for example, could mean either "product" or "profit." Is the net product or the net profit being distributed unequally? Period dictionaries may be of some help in this determination. Economic polyglot glossaries are also essential. A sixteenth-century dictionary may be more accurate than a twentieth-century edition, despite the fact that two centuries separate both from the period in question, since there has been more rapid language evolution between the eighteenth century and the twentieth than between the sixteenth and the eighteenth centuries. The best source may be a renowned translation of a work dealing with similar subject matter. This, of course, means comparing texts, a tedious, time-consuming chore.

Fermier is a term which appears and reappears. Cursorily, we might render this as "farmer." Undoubtedly, the term thus translated is over general, even incorrect. *Fermier*, rather, refers to a tenant farmer or sharecropper. The latter is often a culturally defined American term; therefore, tenant farmer may be the preferred option. The agrarian hierarchy of the eighteenth century was complex and fluid. Different

84

texts will group subdivisions of this scale in different social orders. This complicates the task of the translator.

Officier may be defined as "civil servant" in the dictionary. This, however, is an anachronism. For lack of a better term, the translator may use civil servant, footnoting the obvious anachronistic flaw.

One further example will illustrate the difficulty which a single term might present. In a discussion of the physiocratic approach to taxation, the phrase *principe censitaire* is encountered. Abridged dictionaries list the term as colloquial. In the Grande Larousse we find that as a noun *censitaire* might mean "1) celui qui devait le cens au seigneur possédant un fief; 2) nom que l'on donne aux citoyens qui payent la quotité d'impôt nécessaire pour jouir des droits électoraux, d'après la loi de leur pays." The first meaning historically precedes the eighteenth century. The second is viable, and we glean the connotation of a poll tax of some sort. As an adjective, we find that *censitaire* means: "1) qui paye le cens; 2) qui paye la quotité d'impôt nécessaire pour être élu ou électeur - les députés censitaires sont plus ou moins aristocrates." This complicates the decision, since we now have the additional possibility of an elected officer, as opposed to a voting citizen. Rechecking the context in which the phrase appeared we find that there is reference to an agrarian hierarchy of wealth. We thus decide to render the term as "progressive poll tax," incorporating elements of the context with the dictionary definitions. However, in continued reading on the subject, we come across a note which states that the physiocratic tax principles were often mistakenly interpreted to mean a system of progressive poll tax. The picture is now further obscured. Did the author of the text in question himself fall prey to this apparent misconception? Or was he properly using the term to denote another concept? Calls to the departments of history and Romance languages led to the choice of "the principle of property assessment." Further thought indicated that further research was called for. In rereading texts on the Physiocrats, particularly those chapters dealing with taxation, the final translation became: "the principle of a direct proportional tax on the *produit net* or on the land." This was footnoted, directing the reader to sources for additional clarification.

There are many decisions which require this type of research—thinking and rethinking a term, comparison of texts, and often, just common sense. Other decisions are more arbitrary. The phrase *Ancien*

Régime, for example, is capitalized in some texts, but not in others. This would then be up to the individual translator, with consistency remaining the most important consideration. Should weights and measures be "translated" or should an explanatory table be inserted? The translator, considering at all times the intended audience and the minor differences in calculations involved, will ultimately make this decision. One may encounter inconsistencies such as the use of dates from the Napoleonic Calendar interspersed with Roman Calendar dates. The translator may leave these, insert the Roman date parenthetically or in a footnote, or consistently employ the Roman Calendar. The procedure used should be explained in a translator's note. Such notes may also be used in the case of an obscure term which which is best left unchanged within the text itself. For example, the text may refer to an area of France called the French Vexin, but a note may be included to explain this location and the origin of the designation. It is probably wise to follow the numerical sequence of the author's own footnotes, while translator's notes may be marked with asterisks or other symbols. This will allow the reader to compare more readily with the original text.

There are also stylistic considerations in translating scholarly works. In French, for example, literary style is quite acceptable in fields where English journals expect strictly professional style. In Hebrew, academic publications use careful repetitions of facts and formulations of concepts to reinforce notions. In English, such repetitions sound tautological and unwarranted.

Prediction

The social sciences are assuming an increasingly important place in academic curricula. The demand for and the value of translation is therefore ever increasing. We are approaching an era wherein the ivory tower will have to come to terms with the tower of Babel.

NOTES

1. Parts of the Old Testament were originally in Aramaic, specifically Genesis (31:47), Jeremiah (10:11) and sections of Daniel (2:4b-7:28) and Ezra (4:8-6:18). See these topics in the *Encyclopedia Judaica*, vol. 4, (Jerusalem: Keter Publishing House, 1971), p. 381.

The Septuagint (Interpretation septuaginta seniorum, i.e., translation of the 70 elders) is the earliest Greek translation, executed in the third century B.C.E. These topics are covered in the *New Catholic Encyclopedia*, vol. II, (New York: McGraw Hill, 1967) and the *Encyclopedia Judaica*, p. 851. The first Latin translation, Jerome's Vulgate, spanned the years 386-420 C.E., *Judaica*, p. 864. The sequence of Old Testament translations is roughly as follows: Greek (third-second centuries B.C.E.), Aramaic (first century B.C.E. -fifth century C.E.), Syriac (first-third century C.E.), Armenian (fifth century C.E.), Arabic (ninth-thirteenth century C.E.). This information was generously supplied by the American Bible Society in New York City.

According to Nida, the Bible had been translated into 1,393 languages as of 1968. See Eugene A. Nida and Charles R. Taber, *The Theory and Practice of Translation* (Leiden: E.J. Brill, 1974), p. vii. According to the American Bible Society, as of December 1977 the *complete* Bible had been translated into 266 languages, the *complete* Old Testament in two more, and the *complete* New Testament into 418 more languages. Parts of these are now available in over 1600 languages according to a recent letter (9/21/79) from this society.

2. A Library of Congress search reveals that prior to 1956, there were 4,320 translations of Homer's works. Since that date, there have been 242 translations in 22 languages.

3. Michael Jasenas, "Translation Sources in the Humanities" in *Translation in the Humanities*, ed. Marilyn Gaddis Rose, (N.Y.: State University of New York at Binghamton, 1977), p. 38.

4. Karl Marx has been translated into 36 languages and well over 500 translations exist. Max Weber has been translated into eight languages and over 50 translations of his works have been rendered. (Source: Library of Conress Catalog)

5. John Easton: 30 translations in 8 languages
Arnold Toynbee: 47 translations in 15 languages
William James: 64 translations in 15 languages
Paul Samuelson: 20 translations in 8 languages
Margaret Meade: 30 translations in 4 languages
Talcott Parsons: 10 translations in 4 languages
John Dewey: 74 translations in 13 languages
(Source: Library of Congress Catalog)

6. William Riker: 1 translation into Spanish
Marc Bloch: 12 translations in 3 languages
Abraham Maslow: 8 translations in 4 languages
Milton Friedman: 2 translations in 2 languages
Radcliffe Brown: 5 translations in 4 languages
Edwin Schur: 1 translation into Italian
John Rawls: no recorded translation
(Source: Library of Congress Catalog)

On the whole, these figures substantiate the claim, Parsons being the single exception.

7. George Steiner, *After Babel* (New York: Oxford University Press, 1975), chapter 5. See also a more complete version of this notion as expounded by Marilyn Gaddis Rose, *Translation in the Humanities*, pp. 1-4.

8. Nida calls it the receptor language. See Nida and Taber, *Theory and Practice*.

Concepts in the Social Sciences:
Problems of Translation

by Immanuel Wallerstein

The translator of materials in the social sciences confronts a difficulty which is perhaps peculiar to the social sciences and is absent, or at least less salient, in translation in literature on the one hand and in mathematics and the physical sciences on the other hand.

A social science text utilizes concepts as the central mode of communication. The concepts are more or less clearly defined and applied by the author. On the one hand they are shared references of meaning, shared summations of data or classifications of reality. Were they not shared with some others, the text would be gibberish. On the other hand, these concepts are not *universally* shared and are quite often the subject of open and violent conflict. In order to translate a concept well, the translator must know (a) the degree to which any concept is in fact shared (and by whom), both at the time of writing and at the time of translation, and (b) the variations of sharing-communities in each of the two languages. The translator should also be able to infer the author's perception of the degree of sharing—that is, whether or not he is aware of or willing to acknowledge the legitimacy of debate over the concept itself.

This is a tall order, and there are virtually no reference volumes which can offer such information. A dictionary, even the best, is by and large of very little assistance. Encyclopedias occasionally are more useful. But essentially the only way to acquire this knowledge is to have read widely in the subfield and to have done this reading in both languages. Needless to say, if the text reflects an innovative thrust, especially one which centers around the redefinition of the concepts themselves, the translator is even more hard pressed, since the acquisition of appropriate background knowledge may have to be from obscurer sources than usual.

Ideally, therefore, the translator must be someone not merely skilled in translation as a generalized technique but familiar with the literature of the subfield over a long period of time, and preferably someone with a direct interest in the material under discussion in the text. This ideal will never be realized until we move towards the creation of a body of translators specialized in the social sciences and trained in both translation techniques and social science. I shall not discuss here the organizational prerequisites for creating such a cadre of persons. Suffice it to say they do not now exist. Most translation in the social sciences is done either by social scientists who are not very good as translators, or by translators with a primary background in literature rather than in social science.[1] The results are by and large appalling (with some notable—but rare—exceptions, to be sure).

I shall address myself here primarily to laying down some simple ground rules for the translator.

(1) Search for the standard translation, if one exists.

By standard translation, I mean the accepted equivalent in the two languages of a technical term. In recent years, international organizations, required to do rapid translations of documents into a series of "official" languages, have begun to publish glossaries. These are very useful, but usually only for terms likely to be utilized in current international debates, treaties, etc. "Standard" also may mean standard for a subgroup of persons to which the author of the text belongs, or about whose ideas he is writing.

Let me give a simple example. I came across the English word "overtime" used as a translation of the French term *surtravail*. This is simply wrong. One can see what happened: the translator did not recognize the term *surtravail* and tried to puzzle out its probable meaning, coming to "overtime," which has a certain prima facie plausibility.

Wondering why the translator did not use a dictionary for such a common term, I looked up the term first in Harrap's largest French-English dictionary, and then in the Grand Robert. *Surtravail* is in neither. Nonetheless, it is one of the central terms of Marxism, and is used in thousands of publications annually. Its standard English equivalent is "surplus labor," and both the English and the French are derived from the German original, *Mehrarbeit*. There is apparently no reference volume which will give you this simple piece of knowledge. Yet any translator who in fact used any term other than "surplus labor" to translate *surtravail* would destroy the meaning of the sentence, perhaps of the paragraph.

Let me now give an example of a standard translation absolutely elementary for any scholar of medieval studies, but very easy to get wrong for a translator who is unaware of a peculiar convention. Historians normally divide the Middle Ages into two periods. In English, we use the locution "Early and Late Middle Ages." The various Germanic languages use parallel terms. For example, in German, we say *Fruh- und Spätmittelalter*. A translator from Spanish will be forgiven if, coming upon the phrase *baja Edad Media*, he/she assumes that low equals early. In fact, the contrary is true. The convention in all the romance languages is that early/late equals high/low. In order to get this right, the translator must first be aware that this curious anomaly may exist. If the translator then seeks to verify suspicions by using dictionaries, I fear the results will be very frustrating. Eventually, the use of bibliographies which translate the words into dates will provide the evidence.

Let me now give a harder example. There is a term central to the ideas of Max Weber, and of all those in the social sciences (very many, indeed) influenced by him. The term is *Stand*. Weber took the term, which had been the classic term for a medieval Estate (that is, a social stratum juridically classified), and extended it in his writings to mean any grouping in any social system that was based on nonmarket-related, nonpolitical criteria. Thus, a religious group could be a *Stand*; so could a racial or ethnic group, etc.

We immediately have a problem in English. We must recognize in a German text whether *Stand* is being used in the classic, restricted sense or in the extended, Weberian sense. If it is the former, we translate *Stand* as "Estate" (carefully capitalizing it). If it is the latter, there has grown up a convention that we translate it with the term "status-group." Since the bulk of American social scientists know the term "status-group" and very few of them read German, if a new German text using *Stand* in the Weberian sense were translated by any term other than "status-group," it would fail to communicate the sense of the author.

There is a further complication with *Stand* if one is translating into

90

or from French. Since Weber's works have never had the intellectual impact in France they have had in the United States, there exists no standard French translation for *Stand* in the extended sense. Some French authors use *Etat*, thus reproducing in French the German confusion (indeed, adding a third, since *Etat* in French not only means "Estate" and "status-group" but also "state"). However, other French authors (and translators into French), seeking to avoid the conceptual confusion, use the German original. Still others use the English term "status-group." Since there are some new translations of Weber into French, there may soon grow up a new convention.

This poses one final complication. Suppose there emerges in French a new term which becomes the standard equivalent of "status-group." Suppose that at this later point in time, someone decides to translate a French text into English written before the new standard convention will have been instituted. In this case, the French text will have utilized the term *Etat*, meaning by it "status-group." In this hypothetical case, our translator, working 20 years from now, would probably have to know not only the history of the concept but also the history of translating conventions in three languages in order to discern that *Etat* should be translated as "status-group."

Finally, a word on standard translations, not of concepts, but of passages. There are some authors who are widely translated and widely cited in many languages—for example, the Bible, Plato, Descartes, Marx, or Freud. If a particular German text which one is translating contains a quotation from Freud in the original German, it is unwise for the translator to hazard a new translation of the Freud citation, since the English reader may only "recognize" the quotation in the already familiar English version. This is particularly true if the passage is a famous one. It is better for the translator to spend time on the library research involved in locating the standard translation than on redoing it. Since one usually needs the texts in both languages to locate the standard translation of the passage, this may, of course, be extremely difficult. If, for example, an Italian text cites Marx's *Das Kapital* in its Italian translation, the translator working in the United States may be able to locate the English and German editions, but the Italian edition may well be unfindable. If the Italian author merely gave a page (as opposed to a chapter) reference, finding the equivalent passage in English without the Italian editions at hand may be next to impossible, and the translator may have to engage in retranslation; this, however, should only be a very last resort.

(2) If the best translation seems either to be anachronistic or to miss a nuance, the solution is to add the original in parentheses.

I offer two examples. In an Italian text dealing with the sixteenth century, the phrase *gli enti morali* may be found, referring to various private institutions engaging in welfare activities. A possible translation would be "nonprofit associations," or, more narrowly, "charitable organizations," by analogy to terminology used in the twentieth-century United States. It seems to me that the original in parentheses is essential because of the anachronism.

There are cases where the issue is not anachronism but the nonexistence of parallel institutions in countries of different languages. In early modern England, the term "yeoman" referred to a land-utilizer with a certain legal status. There was no equivalent legal concept in France. In northern France, in turn, the term *laboureur* referred to a land-utilizer who owned a particular type of plow known in French as a *charrue*. This is to be distinguished from a less heavy plow known as an *araire*, although both terms are frequently translated into English simply as "plow." In fact, and this is my substantive analysis, the northern French *laboureur* and the English "yeoman" were more or less parallel in their social role, their control of the land, the size of their plots, and the level of their wealth. One might therefore legitimately translate *laboureur* as "yeoman," but certainly not without the original in parentheses.

(3) If a concept is standard in one language, but not (or not yet) in the other, either do not translate, or indicate to the reader the existence of this intellectual difference between the two linguistic cultures.

In a recent translation of Giovanni Arrighi's *The Geometry of Imperialism*, Patrick Camiller, the translator, coming to the phrase, *in modo univoco* translated it as "a univocal representation" and then added a translator's note:

> The term "univocal representation", used throughout *The Geometry of Imperialism*, is taken from the epistemology of Galvano Della Volpe, as

is "historically determinate definition". For an account of the meaning of "univocal" here, see Galvano Della Volpe, *Critique of Taste*, NLB, London 1978, Chapter Two.[2]

What the translator has done here is to recognize that the reader who is unfamiliar with Della Volpe may invent in his mind a meaning for "univocal representation" far from what the author (Arrighi) intended to convey. Of course, a translator unfamiliar with Della Volpe would have been incapable of adding this crucial note. Once again, recourse to any dictionary would have been futile.

In French historical literature of the past 25 years, the trinity *structure, conjoncture, événement*, intended to represent three different social times, has been widely used. The translator might, however, encounter these concepts not as a trinity of nouns but as mere adjectives, the author assuming acquaintance with the trinity. The adjective *conjoncturel* might indeed appear alone, or perhaps paired with either *structurel* or *événementiel*. No standard translation now exists for the nouns and even less for the adjectives. Some translate the trinity as "structure, conjuncture, event." But others note that the dictionary meaning of "conjuncture" in English is radically different from the use of *conjoncture* in this trinity. The French term *conjoncture* as used here refers to a 15-30 year trend either upward or downward along some curve, whereas the English term "conjuncture" normally refers to a meeting-point in time of different forces—nearer in fact to the French *événement*, although not quite. In this case, an appropriate translation depends on the particular context, but unless the translator is firmly grounded in the conceptual distinctions among social time underlying the use of the particular adjective, he/she may well translate a counter-sense.

A third example poses still different problems. Since the late nineteenth century, there has been a distinction in the German literature on agrarian economies between a *Grundwirtschaft* and a *Gutswirtschaft*. It refers to the fact that, on some estates in the Germanic lands between the sixteenth and nineteenth centuries, the landlord received all or most of his income in the form of rent from tenants (*Grundherrschaft*), whereas, on others, the landlord received an important part of his income from direct exploitation for the market of some but not all of the land he owned (*Gutsherrschaft*).

Some have sought to render this distinction as one between a "manor economy" and a "demesne economy." The problem is that this is not a familiar distinction in English, largely because in the real world of English agriculture the distinction scarcely existed in the form it existed in in Germanic lands. Therefore, using these English terms might confuse even experts, especially if one used only one of them (such as "semesne economy" to translate *Gutswirtschaft*). Furthermore, the meaning of the two terms in German has been the subject of an enormous and heated debate among German scholars. In recent years, some of them have attempted to insert a third or intermediate concept called *Wirtschaftsherrschaft*. I suspect that in this minefield, where Germans are debating the meaning of German concepts and we have no good English equivalents, there is no alternative but to use the German original in the literature. This is, in fact, widely done. Once again, a translator stumbling onto an adjectival variant such as *grundherrlichen* would have no intelligent way of handling the problem without absorbing a considerable part of the substantive debate into his/her own fund of knowledge.

(4) If a term which does have a standard translation is used by the author in a markedly different way which is understandable in the original context, do *not* translate with the standard term.

The French verb *franciser* is defined in the Grand Robert as meaning "to give a French expression to (a foreign expression)" or "to give a French character to (something)." The English word "Gallicize" might be considered a standard translation. It can, in fact, be found as the translation in Harrap's. If, however, the French author is writing about the linguistic distinction in France between the *langue d'Oïl* and the *langue d'Oc*, then *franciser* means to shift an area linguistically from Oc to Oïl. To translate this use of *franciser* as "to Gallicize" is to miss the whole point. Since this is an issue rarely discussed in English-language literature, no equivalent exists for this use of *franciser* and no obvious neologism springs to mind. In this case, the use of the French original with a translator's note is one possible solution.

Another example is *Staatswissenschaften*. Literally, this means "sciences of the State." As a term, it was used in Germany in the late nineteenth and early twentieth century to cover a set of research

94

activities that included legal and constitutional history, comparative analysis of agrarian economies, sociological theory, political philosophy, and many other topics. To define it is to discuss the intellectual history of Germany in comparison to that of France and England. It might be translated "social sciences," except that the term "social sciences" makes certain assumptions about the grouping of intellectual concerns which is different from the term *Staatwissenschaften*. In contemporary Germany, the term *Sozialwissenschaften*, a literal translation from the English, has been adopted to designate "Social Sciences." I believe, therefore, that when *Staatswissenschaften* is used in the sense of designating a distinctive grouping of knowledge different from the English grouping, it is untranslatable and should be left in the original. When, however, it is used as the equivalent of "social sciences," it should be so translated. This requires the translator to make a substantive judgment about the viewpoint of the author, especially for works written in the 1920s, a period of transition in usage.

There is further complication. In contemporary Norway, the word *Statsvitenskap* is used to mean "political science" (in the United States usage). The Norwegians have simply redefined a term they took over from the German *Staatswissenschaft* before the first World War. If the author is using *Statsvitenskap* in a contemporary context, the standard translation would be "political science." If, however, the author is using the term in the sense of the old German usage, then the only intelligible translation from Norwegian to English would be to use the German term *Staatswissenschaft* in English.

(5) If a term has different cognitive ranges in the two languages, and the concept is central to the article, the translator ought to indicate that, either by a note or by a parenthetical use of the original term.

Compare the French term *chef d'exploitation* and the English term "farmer." Both are nonspecific and cover a wide variety of social roles. Farmer is most frequently used to speak of anyone who cultivated land, whether owner or tenant, and sometimes even includes the farm laborer. In some usages, it may include an absentee landlord as well. There is no equivalently broad expression in most European languages.

However, the French expression *chef d'exploitation* also covers a broad, if somewhat different, range. Anyone who controls the decision-making processes on a unit of agricultural production is a *chef d'exploitation*. In this case, I believe the two terms are near enough to be used for each other, when intended in their broad senses, but not without some indication by the translator to the reader of what has happened in the translation.

(6) If a term has different cognitive ranges *within* both languages but parallel between the languages, the safest bet is literal translation, preferably by use of cognates if they exist.

A good example is the term "bourgeoisie." In the analysis of the social structure of medieval Europe that has prevailed since the late eighteenth century, "bourgeoisie" is the term used to designate a middle social stratum located between the "aristocracy" and the "peasantry." In the analysis of the social structure of the nineteenth and twentieth centuries, "bourgeoisie" is used by many writers to designate the top social stratum. Some writers consequently use the term "middle strata" or "middle classes" to designate those socially located between the "bourgeoisie" and the "proletariat" or the "working classes."

The result is that there is a permanent ambiguity in social science literature about the relation of the terms "bourgeoisie" and "middle classes." Sometimes they are meant as synonyms; sometimes they are meant to designate distinct groups. Some authors are sloppy about the ambiguity—unconsciously or deliberately. The translator should never impose order where there is no order, or where order is not wanted. Hence to translate *la bourgeoisie* as "the middle classes" (and conversely *les classes moyennes* as "the bourgeoisie") risks altering, sometimes fundamentally, the sense the author is seeking to convey.

Another example is "nobility" and "aristocracy." In the usage of most authors, they are virtually identical terms. Some analysts refuse to accept the legitimacy of any conceptual distinction. Others, however, use the terms to designate two different groups, the nobility being lesser landowners than the aristocracy. In many writings, it is not clear whether the author intends a distinction or not. Once again, literal translation is the best solution.

(7) When an author seeks to undo conceptual confusion, the translator must not restore it.

This is perhaps the most difficult task of all. Every once in a while, an author seeks to cut through a morass of conceptual confusion among the best scholars in the field either by using a standard term in a new way, or by inventing a neologism. The author may not, however, blow a trumpet to announce this fact; rather he/she may simply do it. The translator must know enough of the field to know that there exists conceptual confusion—or at least that the author thinks there does— and also perceive that the author is using an old term in a new way or inventing a neologism in order to resolve the confusion. In such a case, it is the translator's obligation to let the author do what the author wants. The translator should not defend the purity of the language of translation against neologisms, but has the obligation to invent a parallel neologism. Nor must the translator defend classic usages against the author's new usage, since the new usage is precisely the author's objective.

I have tried to emphasize the practical problems of social science translation and to reiterate some homespun truths, such as the limited utility of dictionaries and the desirability of intelligent self-effacement (or intellectual noninterference) on the part of the translator. Above all, I have tried to convey the reality of social science: that the concepts on which it is based are its foundation, but that this is a foundation which is constantly shifting because of social (and consequently intellectual) conflicts. The translator cannot intelligently translate unless he/she knows where the author comes from, with whom the author is arguing, and what others (the author's contemporaries, the translator's contemporaries) think of the concepts the author is using. There is no way a translator can approach a piece of writing cold and do a first-rate job of translation in the social sciences. The translator first must be an informed, indeed a very well-informed, reader of the author. In my view, the translator cannot become so informed merely by reading some books at the time of the translation in order to facilitate that particular translation. Being well-informed is a process of slow and long-term prior acquisition of substantive knowledge. Translators of social science must be specialized social scientists as well as translators.

IMMANUEL WALLERSTEIN

NOTES

1. This is not in fact true when the translation is from a language outside the main contemporary European ones. A translation into English from Arabic, or Old Norse, or medieval Latin is usually the work of a scholar in the field, who will often discuss in the footnotes the problems of translating the concepts. I am referring here to translations of modern materials among present-day Romance, Germanic, and Slavic languages.

2. (London: New Left Books, 1978), p. 32.

Translation from the Classics

by Zoja Pavlovskis

With the exception of intractable documents such as funerary inscriptions, contracts, treaties, personal messages, graffiti, and the like, all of them immensely valuable to the historian and often entertaining to the layman but never intended to please aesthetic sensibilities, the bulk of classical texts that always have been—and no doubt always will be—translated into other languages is composed of literary works.[1] The former class of writings is arguably best left untranslated, since the professional archaeologist, numismatist, or epigrapher, who is frequently the only person capable of correctly dealing with them and evaluating their significance for the rest of the world, is in all conscience bound to acquaint himself with the original document in its original state: its wording, spacing, spelling; even the gaps, mistakes, and other shortcomings it may possess can allow a specialist to ascertain its period, the literacy and social class of its author, the physical conditions under which it was fashioned, be it with chisel and stone or pen and papyrus. The smallest dot on a piece of parchment, the least conspicuous scratch on a bronze plate may be of import in this sort of study and will be disregarded only at the risk of losing—or perhaps never gaining—a reputation. Translation, and even transcription, cannot suffice. The nonspecialist must accept the experts' opinion or, if he is bewildered by disagreements among them and cares enough about the subject, will have to become an expert in his own right.[2]

An error in literary translation is, of course, also perilous to its perpetrator; yet in this area the quality of the finished product has traditionally carried more weight on the critic's scale than philological exactitude manages to earn. Whether he does it intentionally or inadvertently, a Virgil can afford to misconstrue Theocritus,[3] and an Ezra Pound is allowed to get away with perverse misinterpretation of

Propertius.[4] Ideally, it takes a poet to translate a poet, but as a corollary of this principle we must necessarily add that a considerable latitude, indeed license, must be accorded to such a version if the translator's own originality is to remain unimpaired. The stronger a poet's individuality, the less likelihood that his translation of another's work will be a mirror reflection. However, common sense suggests that there is a point of no return in the process: past it, the re-creation of a work can no longer be called translation but instead becomes another scion in a possibly large grove of books that belong to the same literary tradition. Pope's *Iliad*, even though it bears a strong imprint of his style, is a translation; his *Essay on Criticism*, no matter how strikingly indebted to Horace's *Ars Poetica*, is a poem with an identity all its own. Must we assign a greater value to the one at the expense of the other? Each represents an important achievement and is enjoyable, and a very large portion of Western literature belongs, or is indebted, to translations from the classics as well as freer adaptations of ancient models.

If defined broadly enough, so as to include such adaptations, the process of transferral (for that is what the word translation denotes) can be viewed as one of the most essential and characteristic features of classical Greek and Roman civilizations, especially the latter—and free definitions of translation frequently are used by critics of the process. Of these, the convenient system for classifying varieties of translation that appears in Roman Jakobson's celebrated essay is probably more applicable to the ancient period than to any other: one can sustain the assertion that classical antiquity, unusually dependent upon translation as Jakobson understands it, exhibited the greatest virtuosity in its application that the world has ever seen. As the student of the subject will easily recollect, Jakobson distinguishes among three kinds of translation: (1) from language to language, (2) within a language, and (3) between media.[5] All three are inseparable from the classics; let us see how they operate in the context of ancient literature and art.

Without the first of these, Latin literature is unthinkable. Ever since Livius Andronicus' awkward but dignified rendition of the *Odyssey*,[6] almost the entire body of writings left to us by the Romans consists of more or less close reworkings of Greek models; the readers of these imitations are expected by their authors to possess a knowledge of the originals and to recognize and admire their transformation in the text

100

they are reading. The modern Romantic concept of total originality would be completely out of place in the framework of classical literature. Catullus[7] and Horace,[8] poets of the highest caliber, do not hesitate to offer to their audience poems, large sections of which are practically literal translations of Sappho and Alcaeus. The ethos of the Roman versions, however, is different: not only does the Latin of Catullus sound more vigorous than the mellifluous dialect of Sappho's native Lesbos but, quite unlike his predecessor, Catullus ends a description of violent physical anguish caused by jealousy with a moralizing passage that would be foreign to Sappho. An appreciation of the differences as well as the similarities between model and imitation is, and is meant to be, basic to our enjoyment of the latter; to fulfill this expectation on the part of an ancient author we must be able, if not to translate, then at least to judge the merits of a good, creative translation when we see one.

These reflections bring us to Jakobson's second point. Model-conscious antiquity diligently studied the older authors and kept their language alive, so that Homer, for instance, did not need to be translated into the Greek of 200 A. D. in order to be understood in that period, the way *Beowulf* has to be put into modern English for us. But for the same reason—reverence for their prototypes—poets, and prose writers too, vied with one another in rewording, paraphrasing, amplifying, reinterpreting, condensing, parodying, and commenting on what their forerunners had produced. The three Electra plays of Aeschylus, Sophocles, and Euripides furnish perhaps the most obvious example of such practices, but scores of other, similarly dependent, works are conspicuous in the extant body of ancient literature, not to speak of passages, characters, or sentiments that can be traced through a long procession of authors and books back to Homer and in the other direction down to our own times. A literal application of the word "translation" is inappropriate here, but if we bear in mind how dissimilar several different modern versions of *Beowulf* can be, and how each of them interprets the old epic in a totally different way, we shall be ready to admit, perhaps, that in a broad sense Sophocles and Euripides can be regarded as translators of Aeschylus—and of each other—and that all three can be considered highly original "translators" of a traditional myth.[9]

Transferral of material between different media also abounded in antiquity, and continued into modern times. Especially noteworthy is the ceaseless preoccupation of ancient (and subsequent) pictorial artists with the same themes and figures that loomed large in the poets' domain. Many a vase painter was inspired by the Homeric epics or by a play he may have seen in the theater[10]; but often it was the poet or the orator who took his inspiration from painting or sculpture, and a special subgenre of classical literature, the *ekphrasis*,[11] owes its existence almost entirely to the practice of emulating in literature the more concrete accomplishments of the visual arts—albeit frequently imaginary ones.

We see, then, that translation of the classics did not begin after the languages of the ancient Greeks and Romans fell into disuse but accompanied and in many ways furthered the growth and development of ancient literature. Nor did this broader kind of transfer from art to art, and from one writer's idiom into another's ever cease: a line of descent is ultimately traceable from Exekias and his fellow artists to Rubens and Delacroix, and from Virgil's models to Milton and Joyce. In the classical tradition, myth provides stronger cohesion than language, yet language too is of supreme importance. In one form or another, the classics will survive, but those who love them would like to ensure a permanence of the identity they see and cherish in each individual work, in addition to metempsychosis into something that, no matter how attractive or even great, no longer shows the lineaments of its former self. This is where the task of translation in the more literal sense begins: accurate, faithful rendition of a text from one language into another in such a way that the replica should turn out to be as like the original as human limitations and the peculiarities of the two languages can allow.

The former of these factors need not concern us here since it depends on the talents, knowledge, and application which an individual translator may or may not be able to put to work. The second, however, needs some discussion, particularly since Latin and Greek present their translators with certain problems either absent from more modern periods or at least not so prominent in their literary works that a translator must keep them in mind at every step.

One of these difficulties is a product of the immense gulf that separates our world from that of classical antiquity. The cultural differences between us and an Athenian of 432 B.C. or a Roman of year 1 A.D. are enormous. Allusions to current politics, private scandals, foods, sanitary habits, and the like,[12] which lend great liveliness and a dash of spice to ancient comedy, satire, or oratory, are for the most part meaningless to a modern reader unless he happens to be a classicist; in that case he needs no translation. Should such references be kept archaeologically precise to satisfy the knowledgeable? If so, can a translator hope that the less well informed reader will enjoy going through his version of an ancient masterpiece at a snail's pace, turning aside all the time to look up information in a lexicon? Or should obscure allusions be updated, no matter if anachronistically, to offer the reader an approximation of bygone conditions to what is more familiar? But if our translator should prefer this option, his work, laborious perhaps, time-consuming, as well as dear to him as an expression of his artistic aspirations, will run the risk of becoming outmoded within a very short time: a play of Aristophanes presented in the guise of an antiwar manifesto replete with references to the war in Vietnam will within a mere dozen of years become a literary curiosity instead of what a classic ought to be: a possession for all time.[13]

Still another, related, difficulty is caused by our general loss of touch with many realities of everyday existence such as were not peculiar to antiquity but vitally important to every human being for unbroken millennia up to the beginning of the Industrial Revolution. The average modern reader lacks even a superficial knowledge, and therefore the vocabulary, of weaving, sailing, riding a horse, hunting, threshing, pruning, and a myriad other activities that were known to the earlier reader at least in their larger principles. Because of this deficiency in our upbringing and experience, some of the most beautifully realistic passages in the classics are apt to impress us not by their great simplicity and closeness to life but, quite contrary to the intention of their authors, may easily appear contrived, unduly technical, even absurd. Virgil's *Georgics*, perhaps the most perfect poems ever written, furnish good examples of this difficulty: a contemporary of the poet, even if he happened to be an aristocratic city dweller and had never touched a plow with his own hands, could yet be assumed to know what a plow looked like and how the various seasonal tasks were performed on the farm. Most likely, he had seen farmers (or slaves) at work on his own estate and may well have supervised them directly. Here willingness to introduce anachronisms will be of no help whatsoever: the translator cannot convert Virgilian landscape into Kansas. Tractors won't do. They have their use, but not in poetry that pretends to a direct link with the classical. And even tractors are alien objects to a true Manhattanite who has no personal mental associations that might make agricultural machines meaningful to him in the context of a work of art.

In the realm of ideas the translator is also often perplexed. Latin words such as *religio*, *fides*, *pietas*, or *numen* are either (as is the case with *religio*) very distant in meaning from their English equivalents or lack such equivalents altogether—and understandably, since the God of Biblical monotheism, who presides over the history of the Western world after the decline of ancient paganism, has very little in common with the powers in whom the ancient Roman believed. *Numen* is that which makes a god a god. Obviously one cannot use this awkward explanatory phrase every time one comes across the word. But what else is there to do? To make matters worse, the definition we have just proposed cannot satisfactorily render the sense of every occurrence of *numen*. Yet the translator would be ill advised to leave the word as it stands, for he would risk total incomprehension on the part of his readers. An expression such as *joie de vivre* can be left unexplained; not so *numen*. To interpret the text for his audience, the translator must study the culture that has produced the text, and study it diligently and for a long time, so that *he*, in any event,knows what *numen* means, or what an ancient plow looked like, or how the Athenian assembly punished its members for coming late to a meeting. How he will translate a word, a passage, or an entire work so that his version be at once faithful and comprehensible—this will be up to his inventiveness and common sense; but without adequate study as preparation for his task neither originality nor sense will be of help.

But besides the problems of cultural transfer, the translator from the classics must confront another cluster of difficulties, which he may find even more bothersome. Literary Greek and Latin exhibit a bewildering variety of styles, as well as (in the case of Greek) a wide diversity of dialect. In the earlier period, dialect tended to be used quite naturally because it was a writer's native idiom. Thus Sappho's Greek, very different from that of her contemporary Solon, ought to preserve its mellifluous quality in a translation. Perhaps one can accomplish this, but is it humanly possible to make Sappho sound slightly foreign too, a speaker of English but not the English of the reader?[14] Can Americans tolerate a Sappho who expresses herself in the patois of New Orleans? Yet if we neglect dialectal peculiarities, we do lose some of the original flavor that for an Athenian, let us say, was inherent in Sappho's Lesbic. In later periods the use of dialect became something of a literary affectation, the purpose of which was to place the characters and the action in a world different from that of the reader. Can we transfer this phenomenon satisfactorily? Can we use Aussie slang to establish a similar distance between us and Theocritean shepherds, once the translator has made them speak English?

And what of the consciously archaizing language of the epic, which was, moreover, a stylized conglomerate of several dialects? What of the similarly mixed language of drama? Very occasionally a translator may hope to succeed in rendering a Greek work so as to suggest the layers of dialectal interplay or innuendo present in the work he is translating—Lucian's *The Syrian Goddess*, done by A. M. Harmon as *The Goddesse of Surrye*[15] is a *tour de force*—but to achieve similar effects for the greater part of Greek literature is impossible. And so with styles: because of its great dependence on tradition, all the works of ancient literature are to a considerable extent interconnected. We must know and take into account the sources and the influences on a writer, who in turn serves as one of the sources and influences on someone else. As has been pointed out above, an ancient reader was expected to be well versed in most of the important works of past centuries, and therefore to be alert to imitation, parody, verbal echo. Modern philologists, no matter how learned, can acquire no comparable awareness, since a very large part of ancient literature is lost. So much the greater, then, is the difficulty a translator must face. To be true to Virgil, his rendition of the *Aeneid* must bear the mark not only of Virgil's earlier style in his *Eclogues* and *Georgics* but also of Lucretius—and not only of Lucretius (whose work we have) but of Ennius (most of whose poetry is lost). The correspondences to and differences from Lucretius, Ennius, and the rest of its many predecessors lend the *Aeneid* an additional dimension which is best likened to a literary phenomenon such as T. S. Eliot's use of his sources in *The Waste Land*. How can one afford to lose this dimension? Yet how can one do justice to it? Even when the translator does recognize numerous verbal parallels in the text on which he is working, how is he to reveal them? By making his version echo other people's translations of the related works?

Finally, the translator must bear in mind that Greek and Latin were written to be heard. The ancients did not read with their eyes only but aloud, and it follows that the sound of a classical text is supremely important and ought not to be disregarded in translating. On the other hand, one can argue that, considering our own lack of training in this respect and the resulting insensitivity of modern ears, a translator's failure to re-create the rhythms and sound patterns inherent in an ancient poem or piece of oratory may not be critical, since his readers will hardly be conscious of these deficiencies. In any case, we must admit that something important is lost to them, and it is of little use to allocate the blame and make it rest with the translator or with his readers.

In summing up, we may remark that translation from the classics is, indeed, difficult and, in some of its aspects, impossible. But even in the times of Sophocles or of Horace[16] it was a truism that human beings will not give up in the face of insuperable obstacles. The old adage— *traduttore traditore*—is, alas, irrefutable, but the word *traditore* can be made to bear a double connotation. If the translator is mindful of the etymological connection between "traitor" and "tradition," he can find comfort in the thought that his work continues and contributes to the perennial, unceasing, indispensable activity of handing ever vital, vigorous and invigorating works from one age to the next.

NOTES

1. This category (as different from strictly functional writings) contains much that in the modern period would not be called literature. Even technical texts written in antiquity exhibited as a matter of course considerable literary pretensions. Cicero's treatises on rhetoric are in themselves masterpieces of that art, and a variety of books on subjects ranging from pharmaceutics to horsemanship (*e. g.*, Nicander's *Alexipharmaca* and Xenophon's *On Horsemanship*) aspired to, and often managed to achieve, elegance of style and literary distinction.

2. This is not to deny the value of translating historical documents for students not yet sufficiently advanced to tackle the originals.

3. *Cf.* Virgil *Eclogue* 3. 71 with Theocritus *Idyl* 3. 10-11.

4. See his "Homage to Sextus Propertius."

5. "On Linguistic Aspects of Translation," *On Translation*, ed. Reuben Brower, (New York: Oxford University Press, 1959), pp 232-39.

6. The fragments of Livius are most easily accessible in *Remains of Old Latin*, II, ed.

E. H. Warmington (Cambridge, Ma.: Harvard, Loeb Classical Library, 1936).

7. *Cf.* Catullus 51 with Sappho's ode, which is preserved in the treatise *On the Sublime*, attributed to Longinus.

8. Also *cf.* Horace *Ode* (*Carmen*) 1. 14 with Alcaeus' poem on a ship caught in a storm (fr. Z2 in Denys Page, *Sappho and Alcaeus*, Oxford University Press, 1955).

9. The relative dating of Sophocles' and Euripides' plays on this subject is uncertain, but they both came later than Aeschylus' version.

10. As a matter of fact, Greek vase painting furnishes much valuable evidence to the student of the Greek theater.

11. E. R. Curtius, *European Literature and the Latin Middle Ages*, tr. W. R. Trask (Princeton, N.J.: Princeton University Press, 1953), says much of interest on the *ekphrasis* in antiquity and in the Middle Ages.

12. In the realm of technology, which changed very slowly, topical references remained intelligible longer, unlike, let us say, our allusions to car models are likely to be. However, technological references present their own problems; see below.

13. This classic phrase is Thucydides' (1. 22).

14. Sappho, of course, wrote primarily for her compatriots, whose dialect was also hers. But the Greek of the average Athenian, or Alexandrian, or Roman—in short, almost all of Sappho's later readers throughout the ancient times—differed from hers quite substantially.

15. In Lucian, IV (Harvard, Loeb, 1925). Harmon remarks (p. 337) on his efforts to do justice to Lucian's Herodotean style: "It would be most unfair to Lucian to turn this tale into contemporary English. In order to have the same effect that it had in his own day, and to be really intelligible, it must seem to come from the lips of an ancient traveller. The version here offered seeks to secure that effect through mimicry of Sir John Mandeville. It is true that Herodotus was better known in Lucian's time than Mandeville is known now, and his language seemed less remote. In every other respect, however—in his limited vocabulary, in his simple style, and in his point of view— Mandeville provides a mask uniquely adapted to the part—if only its wearer does not fall down in it and break it."

16. See *Antigone* 332-75; Horace *Carm.* 1. 3.

Metamorphosis of Medieval into Modern

by Sandro Sticca

Literary works of art are normally analyzed as thematic structures that, within determined rules of linguistic and poetic combinations, realize or bring to fruition the artistic potentialities inherent in the particular language. Any critical evaluation of the work of art must, therefore, take into account the organizational structuration of its compositional elements, for the structuration of linguistic material determines in many instances the form and the content of the work of art itself.

Particularly as it concerns the rendering of medieval texts into modern versions, the problem that confronts the translator is that of determining the finality and tonality of the text to be translated. The translator must choose between the significative and the objective reality of the text; he must identify the rapport that exists between the signifier and the signified, between the poetic and the semiotic elements of the text; he must decide to what extent the text must be looked upon as autonomous linguistic material, as the structural realization of linguistic and communicative possibilities independent of its psychological, cultural and social expressivity.

Conscious of the highly synthetic nature of Latin and the erudite Latinity of many writers, the translator has to determine if he can thread a harmonious line in his translation between style and content, in order to produce, like the original, beauty of expression and clarity of communication. Indeed, the translator must be a highly skilled stylist, for he is called upon to render, in his translation, the linguistic modulations and conceptual thematics of such diverse medieval compositions as drama, epistle, didactic poems, satire, homiletic verse, epic, history, lyrics, pastoral, anecdotes, etc.

The task is not an easy one, for in attempting, through translation, to capture the inner essence of the work of art, the translator's interpretation of the text may be distorted by the intellectual character of his mind and by the nature of his own experience. This is particularly true of translations of works far removed from the translator's own culture. In the re-creation of the work of art, the translator must recapture, by operating outside of time and moving freely in time, the artistic unity and essence of the original. The translation, in particular, of medieval works written in Latin involves the discovery of a type of vision of life; it involves the ability on the part of the translator, unaffected by the contingencies of his modern experience and the transitory influences of time, to shape the transformation of a past aesthetic construction into a new aesthetic unity. Medieval writers themselves were conscious of the difficulties inherent in such a task. The Venerable Bede, for instance, who died in 735, writing about the gifted poet Caedmon in his *Historia Ecclesiastica*, states that it is impossible to translate poems word for word from one language into another without loss of decorum and dignity: "neque enim possunt carmina, quamvis optime composita, ex alia in aliam linguam ad verbum sine detrimento sui decoris ac dignitatis transferri."[1]

My aim, within the present context, is to analyze some of the problems and difficulties inherent in translating the Latin works of a prominent medieval writer, Hrotswitha of Gandersheim. Within the mainstream of tenth-century civilization, Hrotswitha deservedly occupies center stage by virtue of her being the earliest and most learned medieval woman poet, the first dramatist after the fall of the ancient classical stage, and the first love poet of the Latin Middle Ages. Hrotswitha's artistic activity, which occurred during the second half of the tenth century, developed in the cultural and intellectual milieu associated with the duchy of Saxony, in which territory was located the Benedictine Abbey of Gandersheim, the cloister where Hrotswitha received her early religious and cultural education. The monastery— the history of which Hrotswitha later recorded in her historical poem *Primordia Coenobii Gandeshemensis*—was founded toward the middle of the ninth century (852) by Duke Liudolf of Saxony and his wife Oda and consecrated in the year 881.

Hrotswitha, who entered Gandersheim in the year 955, was probably born about 935. Although the year of her death is not historically documented, the evidence provided by the *Hildesheim Chronicles*, and that contained within the works themselves, suggest that Hrotswitha must have lived to the end of the century, her death probably occurring between 1001-1003. From information provided by her dedicatory verses, epistles prefaced to different sections of her works, and the works themselves, one learns that Hrotswitha received a sound education in both classical and religious literature. The learning that she acquired within the sacred walls of Gandersheim was both wide and diversified. She appears to have been familiar with Virgil's *Aeneid*, the *Eclogues*, Ovid's *Metamorphoses*, and Terence's comedies; of the Christian writers she appears to have read Prudentius, her most important model (especially his *Peristephanon, Psychomachia* and *Apotheosis*), Sedulius, Venantius Fortunatus, and the great philosopher and statesman of the sixth century, Boethius. She had a thorough training in the *trivium* and in the *quadrivium*, and a mastery of the writing skills, which she confesses to have acquired through a laborious and disciplined study; above all, she was steeped in the large body of hagiographical accounts, especially the *Passiones* and the *Vita patrum*.

The manuscript—Emmeran-Munich Codex—containing all the extent works of Hrotswitha, with the exception of the *Primordia Coenobii Gandeshemensis*, was found in the monastery of St. Emmeran at Regensburg in 1493 by Conrad Celtes, the fifteenth-century humanist who published it in 1501. The manuscript, which paleographical evidence indicates was written between the late tenth and early eleventh century, is presently kept in Munich—Bayerische Staatsbibliothek Clm 14485. Composed entirely in Latin, Hrotswitha's literary works as contained in this manuscript can be divided into three groups: (1) *Eight sacred legends or poems* in leonine hexameters, the first five of which are preceded by a prose preface and a verse dedication to Gerberga II, Abbess of Gandersheim from 959 to 1001, and the last three by an additional dedication to her. (2) *Six dramas* preceded by a preface and a prose introduction, *Epistola eiusdem ad quosdam sapientes huius libri fautores*, which is addressed to her readers. (3) *Two historical poems* in heroic verse arranged within a complex whole that includes a prefatory dedication to Gerberga II, a verse dedication to Otto I and Otto II, the *Gesta Ottonis*, and a verse introduction. In this group belongs Hrotswitha's *Primordia Coenobii Gandeshemensis* which is not included in Munich Clm 14485. Although the monk Heinrich Bodo (1470-1553) attests to the existence of the *Primordia* in manuscript form as early as 1531, this historical poem was first printed in its entirety in Johann Georg Leuchfeld's *Antiquitates Gandersheimenses* (Wolfenbuttel, 1709), pp. 409-426.

Hrotswitha's varied artistic production demands of the translator the re-creation and communication of different modes of thought and expression in rendering into English the movement, tone, and structural complexity of tenth-century Latin employed in the realization of different artistic endeavors. Indeed, the Latin Hrotswitha used in the composition of her eight hagiographical poems and her six dramas is fundamentally spiritual and patristic, deeply colored by her medieval heritage of Benedictinism and rich in liturgical content. In addition, Hrotswitha intermingled reminiscences of classical authors such as Virgil, Ovid and Terence in the dramatic structure of her religious plays. The Latin she utilized in her two historical poems, *Gesta Ottonis* and *Primordia*, however, is more literary and less liturgical, more courtly and less hagiographical, more erudite and less provincial, and not governed by theological preoccupations. The translation of the first two works requires a language which at its best is but an imperfect instrument of the miraculous, a language that must render the ineffable ultimacy of the Christian mystery whose God permeates these works with His sacrosanct presence, a language colored by the allusive, the symbolic, the sacred, the supernatural. The historical poems, on the other hand, are better rendered in translation by a language that is more archaic, literary, rhetorical and courtly. For this reason, therefore, it is quite difficult, in translating the various works of Hrotswitha, to achieve a totally integrated linguistic structure. The translation of some passages from different samples of her works will provide a meaningful crystallization of the problem. At the end of the play *Dulcitius*, as the three Christian virgins' execution is entrusted to Count Sisinnius, Irene, the youngest of them, says to him:

Hinc mihi quam maxime gaudendum, tibi vero dolendum, quia pro tui severitate malignitatis in tartara dampnaberis; ego autem, martirii palmam virginitatisque receptura coronam intrabo aethereum aeterni regis thalamum! Cui est honor et gloria in saecula.[2]

111

The vocabulary, in this passage, is intimately connected with the Biblical tradition, the liturgy and the victorious exaltation of hagiographical accounts. The translation of it, therefore, must render the richness of this salvific language:

> For what will come to pass I shall exceedingly rejoice, you in truth shall sorrow, for the gravity of your wickedness shall damn you into hell; I, having been bestowed the palm of martyrdom and the crown of virginity, shall enter the heavenly dwelling of the eternal King, to Whom be glory and honor for ever and ever.

A passage from the historical poem *Gesta Ottonis* will illustrate, on the other hand, the kind of Latin Hrotswitha used in dramatizing the raw historical material and the political, social, and courtly milieu surrounding it:

> Postquam rex regum, qui solus regnat in aevum,
> Per se cunctorum transmutans tempora regum,
> Iussit Francorum transferri nobile regnum
> Ad claram gentem Saxonum, nomen habentem
> A saxo per duritiam mentis bene firmam,
> Filius Oddonis magni ducis et venerandi,
> Scilicet Henricus, suscepit regia primus
> Iusto pro populo moderamine sceptra gerenda.[3]

The language here is epic in character, chivalric and feudal in tone, better suited for the chronicling of historical events associated with the nobility. The translation needs to be rendered in language reflecting the elegance, the rhetorical movement, the formality, and the encomiastic nature of the original:

> Afterward, the King of kings, Who alone reigns forever,
> Transmuting by His power the time periods of all kings,
> Commanded that the noble kingdom of the Franks be transferred
> Unto the illustrious race of Saxony, so named
> From stone by virtue of the stout severity of their character;
> The son of Otto, the renowned and honourable leader,
> Namely Henry, first undertook to hold the royal
> Scepter for the governing of the just people.

The varied literary reminiscences that shaped Hrotswitha's works demand not only a careful re-creation of the fundamental tone and character of each but require also the re-creation of the different emotional and metaphorical texture of certain passages structured within an otherwise highly unified whole. In *Abraham*, for instance, Hrotswitha's fourth play, rightly considered her crowning poetic achievement, the disciplined and orthodox formalism of the play's drama of sin and salvation is disrupted by the presence of amatory passages which, by their essentially mundane nature, transcend the spiritual dimension of the dramatic narrative. The drama centers on the young virgin Maria, raised into a life of chastity under the guidance of her putative uncle, the hermit Abraham. After having been seduced into sin by an evil monk, Maria's return to a life of grace is achieved through the efforts of Abraham, who visits her in a brothel disguised as a lover, *sub specie amatoris*. The passage in question starts as the holy hermit Abraham asks the brothel's innkeeper to see Maria:

Abraham:	Accipe vile munus, quod defero, et fac, ut praepulchra, quam tecum observari experiebar, puella nostro intersit convivio.
Stabularius:	Cur illam desideras videre?
Abraham:	Quia nimium delector in eius agnitione, cuius pulchritudinem quam pluribus laudari audiebam saepissime.
Stabularius:	Quisquis laudator eius formae extitit, nihil fefellit; nam praenitet venustate prae ceteris mulieribus.
Abraham:	Ideo ardeo in eius amore.
Stabularius:	Miror te in decrepita senectute iuvenculae mulieris amorem spirare.
Abraham:	Percerte nullius rei causa accessi, nisi eam videndi.
Stabularius:	Fortunata Maria, laetare; quia non solum, ut actenus, tui coaevi, sed etiam senio iam confecti te adeunt, te ad amandum confluunt.
Maria:	Quicumque me diligunt, aequalem amoris vicem a me recipiunt!
Abraham:	Accede, Maria, et da mihi osculum.
Maria:	Non solum dulcia oscula libabo, sed etiam crebris senile collum amplexibus mulcebo.

It is quite obvious that this is not the patristical, biblical and liturgical Latin reflecting sacramental, catechistic, and redemptive concerns; it is rather the sensual and passionate kind of Latin reminiscent of the seductive and erotic ratiocination of Ovid's *Ars amandi* and *Remedia amoris*, and of the romantic and courtly Latin love poems of the early Middle Ages. The tone of the passage would have to be rendered thus:

Abraham:	Accept the humble present I bear, and allow that most beautiful girl who lodges in your house to have supper with me.
Innkeeper:	Why would you like to see her?
Abraham:	For I greatly delight to know her; I have often heard her beauty praised by many.
Innkeeper:	Whoever extolled her beauty was not at all mistaken. Her striking loveliness outshines all other women.
Abraham:	That is why I am burning with love for her.
Innkeeper:	I am astonished that a decrepit old man like you should yearn for the love of a young girl.
Abraham:	In truth, I have come precisely to feast my eyes
Innkeeper:	You are fortunate, Maria! For not only lovers as young as you flock to your arms but wise old men
Maria:	Whoever loves me I shall love in like manner.
Abraham:	Come nearer, Mary, and give me a kiss.
Maria:	I shall bestow on you sweet kisses and, in tight embraces, stroke your neck.

At this crucial amatory moment, the holy hermit reveals himself to Mary and brings about her repentance.

The translation of these various Latin passages reveals that the complex density of thought in Hrotswitha's works demands not only an understanding of the total actuality and singularity of each particular work but also of the specific emotion inherent in given passages within each work. The use of a conventional mode of translation structured about a uniformly even language would be a meaningless linguistic and literary exercise. Hrotswitha's works, as a whole, are characterized by an architectural centrality, a disciplined and structured aesthetics which is achieved through a perfectly integrated relationship between literary concerns and the theological or religious doctrine upon which they are built. Yet this complex sacramental poetics demands, at times, the full exploitation, in translation, of the language's resources to communicate the varying nuances of her Latin, which is used to describe religious fervor and epic grandeur, ineffable mysticism and sensual rhetoric, biblical exegesis and mere mortality.

NOTES

1. Bede, *Historia Ecclesiastica*, in K. P. Harrington, ed., *Medieval Latin* (Chicago: University of Chicago Press, 1962), p. 88: "Indeed poems, although carefully composed, cannot be translated word for word from one language into another without loss of decorum and dignity."
2. Paulus de Winterfeld, *Hrotsvithae Opera* (Berolini: Weidmannos, 1965), p. 134.
3. Ibid., p. 305.

The Writer as Translator:
Nerval, Baudelaire, Gide

by Haskell M. Block

Translators have not often been great writers in their own right. Understandably, the claims of one's own creations almost always take precedence over those of others, and while writers may sometimes essay the role of the translator, they do so generally as an incidental way of developing their own talents or as a tribute to a much admired predecessor. Not very many major writers have been so committed to translation as to view the enterprise as a central part of their literary calling. Where such sustained activity has been the concern of writers of uncommon talent, it has resulted in some of the great translations of world literature.

All national literatures can offer examples of writers as translators. French literature is not unique, either in its critical and reflective tendencies or in its array of great translators, but in view of the contribution that French writers have made to our literary heritage, French examples of the writer as translator should be of more than ordinary interest. I have selected Nerval, Baudelaire, and Gide for illustrative purposes in the hope that their engagement as translators can help us better understand translation itself as a literary art. All three writers have other and larger claims on our attention, but their achievement as translators is no small indication of their artistry.

We are gradually coming to recognize Gérard de Nerval as one of the major figures of modern literature. The awareness of the complexity and power of Nerval's oneiric vision is in large part the consequence of recent scholarship and criticism, and it has led to a new appreciation of all of his literary efforts. His translation of part one of Goethe's *Faust* was published in Paris in 1828, when Nerval was only twenty. Two years later he brought out a volume of German lyric poetry, and in 1840, he published a version of the second part of *Faust* along with his earlier translation. In the 1840s, Nerval's most important preoccupation as a translator was the poetry of Heinrich Heine. Nerval's activity as a translator extends over the greater part of his career. While his translations were made in part out of economic necessity, he pursued translation as a literary art and was seriously concerned with theoretical as well as practical aspects of translation.

Nerval's version of part one of *Faust* is recognized to this day as one of the great French translations, yet Nerval realized that all translation must be an approximation, especially so when poetry is in question. In the preface to *Faust* in 1828, Nerval contends that a satisfactory rendering of Goethe's play simply is not possible. In reviewing the efforts of his predecessors, Sainte-Aulaire and Stapfer, he contrasts the unfaithful but often felicitous version of Sainte-Aulaire with the pedestrian but literal and complete translation of Stapfer. Nerval's aim, he insists, is to be both faithful and literary, yet he recognizes that for *Faust*, this aim is unrealizable, partly for reasons inherent in all translation, but also because of the obscurity and density of the original, "car il est reconnu que *Faust* renferme certains passages, certaines allusions, que les Allemands eux-mêmes ne peuvent comprendre."[1]

While Goethe's *Faust* is marked by a mixture of verse and prose, Nerval's translation is almost wholly in prose, but it captures the spirit as well as the letter of the original. Nerval's version is far superior to a literal translation; his prose is supple, nuanced, and evocative, but it cannot match Goethe's poetry. In a footnote on the *Walpurgisnacht*, Nerval remarks, "Madame de Staël avait eu raison, sans doute, de proclamer *Faust* une œuvre *intraduisible*."[2] Yet he takes his attempt seriously indeed. Let us look at a few examples. In the famous speech of the Lord to Mephistopheles in the "Prolog im Himmel," Goethe defines the devil's nature and function as follows:

> Du darfst auch da nur frei erscheinen;
> Ich habe Deinesgleichen nie gehasst.
> Von allen Geistern die verneinen
> Ist mir der Schalk am wenigsten zur Last.
> Des Menschen Tätigkeit kann allzuleicht erschlaffen,
> Er liebt sich bald die unbedingte Ruh;

> Drum geb' ich gern ihm den Gesellen zu,
> Der reizt und wirkt and muss als Teufel schaffen.

Here is Nerval's version:

> Tu pourras toujours te présenter ici librement. Je n'ai jemais haï tes pareils. Entre les esprits qui nient, l'esprit de ruse et de malice me déplaît le moins de tous. L'activité de l'homme se relâche trop souvent; il est enclin à la paresse, et j'aime à lui voir un compagnon actif, inquiet, et qui même peut créer au besoin comme le diable.[3]

Apart from a few instances of over-elaboration, Nerval's rendition is close to Goethe's meaning and captures many nuances even if it sacrifices meter and rhyme. Sometimes Nerval can make prose do the work of poetry, as in Mephistopheles' description of himself to Faust in the second study scene:

> Ich bin der Geist der stets verneint!
> Und das mit Recht;...

Nerval translates, "Je suis l'esprit qui toujours nie; et c'est avec justice ..." The translation expresses the same energy of style as the original, and the internal rhyme compensates substantially for the replacement of poetry by prose. It was no doubt for such reasons that Goethe so highly praised Nerval's translation of part one of *Faust* in a conversation with Eckermann early in 1830: "in dieser französischen Übersetzung wirkt alles wieder durchaus frisch, neu und geistreich."[4] We may be sure, however, that Goethe would not have said the same about Nerval's version of part two of *Faust*, published in 1840. Here Nerval reverts to the method of the previously criticized Sainte-Aulaire. Only the third act is translated in its entirety; the other acts are rendered in fragments, with deleted scenes replaced by a summary or *Examen analytique*. In his *Avertissement* Nerval justifies this practice by contending that, except for Act III, part two of *Faust* is not coherently related to the legend and is markedly inferior to part one, despite certain beauties of detail.[5] His translation of part two was probably a hasty attempt to profit from the deserved success of his earlier version.

Nerval's collaboration with Heine in the translation of the latter's poetry is one of the most intriguing literary events of the nineteenth century. It was a rare stroke of fortune that brought two great poets together in a common enterprise. Nerval's command of German was not fluent, and in a letter of 1840 to Heine he complains of his difficulties: "l'admirable richesse de certains détails me laisse parfois dans l'incertitude si je dois germaniser la phrase ou rendre par un équivalent français."[6] Heine's aid must have been precious to his translator. Each poet has left us a tender and warm appreciation of the other's personality and art. Their deep personal and literary affinities are reflected in a similar expression of simple and impassioned lyricism marked by complex and subtle feeling. Heine praised Nerval highly as a translator: "sans comprendre beaucoup la langue allemande, Gérard devinait mieux le sens d'une poésie écrite en allemand, que ceux qui avaient fait de cet idiome l'étude de toute leur vie. Et c'était un grand artiste; . . ."[7] The last point is the most important. Had Nerval not been a great poet, his renditions of Heine would not have had the same imaginative vitality. Despite their many meetings together, when Heine's poetry was collected in French, he noted that Nerval had omitted seven poems from *Die Nordsee*. While he admired Nerval's translations, he complained, as perforce all poets must, "La pensée intime de l'original s'évapore facilement dans la traduction."[8] It could be shown that Nerval made Heine into more of a Symbolist poet *avant la lettre* than the German texts would support, a transposition wholly in keeping with Nerval's own Symbolist anticipations. For Nerval, translation is a creative act, and the translator of poetry must necessarily be himself a poet.

Baudelaire achieved greatness as poet, critic, and translator. The translation of the writings of Poe preoccupied him over a period of 17 years, and while, as for Nerval, there were practical motives for Baudelaire's effort, he was animated primarily by his desire to make Poe and his work known and admired by his countrymen. The close link between Baudelaire's translation and his literary criticism is confirmed by his three substantial essays on Poe. The last of these, "Notes nouvelles sur Edgar Poe," is one of Baudelaire's crucial statements of poetic theory, defining the imagination, *la reine des facultés*, as a synthesizing and symbolizing power. Poe's impact on Baudelaire's critical thought is unmistakable, but W. T. Bandy is surely correct in his view that Poe inspired Baudelaire far more than he influenced him.[9] It would be difficult to contend that Poe is reflected in any significant way in *Les Fleurs du mal*. Yet, as Rémy de Gourmont declared, even if Baudelaire had not written *Les Fleurs du mal*, he would merit a high place in French literature for his translations of Poe. A feeling of personal affinity was a primary force in Baudelaire's dedication to his task. As he remarked in a famous letter of 1864 to Théophile Thoré, "Eh bien! on m'accuse, moi, d'imiter Edgar Poe! Savez-vous pourquoi j'ai si patiemment traduit Poe? Parce qu'il me ressemblait. La première fois que j'ai ouvert un livre de lui, j'ai vu, avec épouvante et ravissement, non seulement des sujets rêvés par moi, mais des PHRASES pensées par moi, et écrites par lui vingt ans auparavant."[10] Baudelaire's discovery points not only to the existence of parallelisms in literature, but to the complexity of the notion of literary originality. It also must have confirmed and reinforced Baudelaire's occult and mystical predilections.

At the beginning of his enterprise Baudelaire evidently did not know English well. His mother was born in England of French parents; she learned English in her childhood, and assisted her son in his studies in the language. Baudelaire seems to have learned English well precisely so that he could translate Poe. His brief remarks in 1848 on the theory of translation indicate a dominant concern with literal exactitude.[11] His passion for accuracy led him to painstaking research as his efforts proceeded. Thus, for the translation of *The Narrative of Arthur Gordon Pym*, he combed the taverns of Paris for an English sailor who could give him the exact meaning of the nautical terms used by Poe.[12] Despite Baudelaire's attention to detail, there are significant lapses in his translations. He tends to confuse tenses so that the conditional in English becomes the future in French.[13] Sometimes he does not grasp idioms or expressions in dialect. Thus, in his version of "The Gold Bug," the black servant's "pale as a gose" is rendered as *pâle comme une oie* instead of ... *un fantôme*.[14] For the most part, however, Baudelaire's translations are both accurate and literary, recapturing the essential qualities of the original. Lapses, where they occur, are often the result of a faulty text or of the carelessness of the copyist or printer.[15]

Baudelaire translated only four of Poe's poems, and it is evident that he had no confidence in the attempt. He seems to have believed that the translation of poetry is impossible. His rendition of "The Raven" is in the manner of the *poème en prose* as a necessary compromise.

Baudelaire's version conveys at least something of the spirit of the original, without the internal rhyme and musicality, as in the refrain: "ce n'est que cela, et rien de plus." No doubt he would have accepted the same necessity for compromise in the translation of his own poetry. In his critical essays, translation is used metaphorically as a description of the poetic process. Thus, in his essay on Victor Hugo, Baudelaire declares, "Or qu'est-ce qu'un poëte ... si ce n'est un traducteur, un déchiffreur?" and in his essay on Wagner he includes the poem, "Correspondances," as a poetic translation of Wagner's music, "la traduction inévitable que mon imagination fit."[16] To write poetry, then, is to translate the mystery of the cosmos revealed in correspondences and analogies. For Baudelaire, the poet is a superior translator.

Gide was among the most wide-ranging of French literary translators. His work included versions of Shakespeare, Blake, Goethe, Pushkin, Whitman, Conrad, Rilke, and Tagore, and extended over the greater part of his long literary career. Similarly to Nerval and Baudelaire, his selections often reflected personal affinities or responses. Evidence abounds in his *Journal* of the seriousness with which Gide approached his own efforts at translation as well as the translations made by others of his own writings. He seems to have enjoyed his activity as a translator but had serious doubts about its validity and complained of the time it took. Thus, after noting in 1917 that his translation of Conrad's *Typhoon* proceeded at the rate of half a page an hour, he added, "je crois que le résultat sera très bon; mais qui s'en apercevra? ... Peu importe."[17] The last offhand remark suggests that Gide approached translation in much the same way as his original compositions. Apart from the personal satisfaction he derived from translating, he also viewed this activity as a critical instrument. He hoped that he would be better able to appreciate Shakespeare by coming to know him through the act of translation.

Gide's long and difficult concern with *Hamlet* is revealing for its illumination of both his theory and practice as a translator. He began the task in 1922 and finished it some 20 years later. An entry in the *Journal* for 14 July 1922 indicates his frustration: "J'achève de traduire, ce matin, le premier acte de *Hamlet*, et renonce à pousser plus avant. J'ai passé trois semaines sur ces quelques pages, à raison de quatre à six heures par jour. Le résultat ne me satisfait pas. La difficulté n'est jamais tout à fait vaincue, et, pour écrire du bon français, il faut quitter trop Shakespeare."[18] Gide's strictures on Shakespeare are not very far from those of Voltaire. After complaining of the infelicities of Shakespeare's style, he adds in the *Journal*: "Je voudrais qu'un Anglais m'en expliquât la beauté." Gide is convinced that Shakespeare must be great, but is not sure why.

Gide seems to have believed that while Shakespeare cannot be adequately translated into French, the attempt is nonetheless worth making. The French translator of Shakespeare, he insists, is forced to sacrifice the poetry in order to convey the meaning. The limits of the French language make the task all but impossible. For Gide, the differences between Elizabethan English and modern French are not literary but structural and fundamental; they cannot be reconciled.[19] One senses a persistent note of despair in Gide's uneasy effort to render the rhythm and movement of Shakespeare's dramatic poetry as well as its thought.

Gide conceived of his version of *Hamlet* as a text that would be both faithful to the original and understandable in the theater. The demands of oral expression as well as the conventions of French dramatic style encouraged him to render Shakespeare in a clear and concentrated idiom. His translation is in straightforward and direct contemporary French, marked by a conscious avoidance of archaisms. This may be exemplified by Horatio's address to the Ghost in Act I

> If thou art privy to thy country's fate,
> Which, happily, foreknowing may avoid,
> O speak!

Gide translates:

> Si tu sais le secret destin de ta patrie,
> si quelque mot de toi, en nous avertissant, peut
> prévenir le sort, oh! parle!

Not only the archaic terms but also the metaphorical density of Shakespeare's language are lost. Gide presents most of the literal meaning, but despite his use of many more words than Shakespeare, he cannot retain "happily" in the second line. Repeatedly in his translation, Gide is obliged to drop phrases of the original and to flatten out the metaphors. We may glance at a portion of Hamlet's

122

famous soliloquy in Act II, Scene ii, beginning "O, what a rogue and peasant slave am I!" as a typical example:

> Am I a coward?
> Who calls me villain, breaks my pate across,
> Plucks off my beard and blows it in my face,
> Tweaks me by th' nose, gives me the lie i' th' throat
> As deep as to the lungs? Who does me this?
> Ha!

Gide translates:

> Suis-je un couard?
> Qui me traitera de lâche? me donnera du
> poing sur la gueule, m'arrachera le poil
> et me souffletera? Qui me tirera par le nez?
> Qui me renfoncera la protestation dans la gorge
> jusqu'au fond des tripes?
> Allons!

Admittedly, these are not easy lines to translate. They are among Shakespeare's most vigorous and liveliest passages, piling verb on verb to relate a series of physical events of mounting intensity. Much of this vigor is lost in the translation by the shift from present to future tense, and by the sheer inability of modern conversational French to recapture the spirit of Elizabethan English. Despite his elongation of phrases, Gide cannot pack all of the meaning in, and is obliged to drop a whole sentence ("Who does me this?") simply to maintain a degree of parity in the lines on the page. The mixed metaphors of Shakespeare are inevitably sacrificed to the clarity and precision of French. Gide constantly flattens out the metaphor by regularizing it.[20] In translating Shakespeare, Gide adapted him to his own literary style. The claims of the original are not wholly abandoned, for Gide is able to retain much of Shakespeare's rhythm as well as meaning, but the clarity and precision of the translation are a direct expression of the literary language employed by Gide in his own writing.[21] Because of the wide variation in affinities, Gide's version of Conrad is distinctly superior to his version of Shakespeare, even though the latter must be considered among the better translations of Shakespeare in French.

Gide's long and dedicated activity as a translator led him to theoretical reflections of broad and general importance, notably in his

"Lettre sur les traductions" of 1928, an essay which no one interested in the theory of translation should overlook.[22] Were he Napoleon, Gide declares, he would require every man of letters in France to translate a foreign work related to his own talents, in the hope of raising the standards of this inadequately rewarded task. The translator for Gide is perforce an artist: "Un bon traducteur doit bien savoir la langue de l'auteur qu'il traduit, mais mieux encore la sienne propre, et j'entends par là non point seulement être capable de l'écrire correctement, mais en connaître les subtilités, les souplesses, les ressources cachées; ce qui ne peut guère être le fait que d'un écrivain professionnel. On ne s'improvise pas traducteur."[23] Too often, Gide insists, translators sacrifice poetic values in both the original and in their own rendition for the sake of literal exactness. It is more important, he declares, to capture the spirit of the original than to reproduce the letter: "... ce n'est pas seulement le sens qu'il s'agit de rendre, il importe de ne pas traduire des mots, mais des phrases, et d'exprimer, sans en rien perdre, pensée et émotion, comme l'auteur les eût exprimées s'il eût écrit directement en français."[24] To satisfy these rigorous and austere criteria, the translation must itself be a work of art. Gide writes out of a lively awareness of the obligation of the writer to be a translator and conversely. His efforts as critic and translator represent a genuine recognition of the importance of translation and of the responsibility of the writer for the enlargement of the literary experience of his countrymen. Underlying Gide's conviction is a profound sense of the necessity of literary cosmopolitanism in a world fragmented by languages and national boundaries.[25] His commitment to translation as a literary art is an expression of his humanistic faith in the spiritual enlargement of peoples through the sharing of their literary heritage.

All of the writers we have discussed were acutely conscious of the artistic demands of translation. Neither Nerval nor Baudelaire were well-known writers at the time they took up translation, but their achievement as translators parallels their more original creative efforts. We have seen in the case of André Gide that his concern with translation came to be a central part of his literary vocation. Nerval and Baudelaire are among the great French translators from Dolet and Amyot to the present day, and Gide at his best is surely one of the foremost French translators of the twentieth century. Their examples suggest that the translator has need of the same imaginative qualities as the novelist, playwright, or poet, and that great translations require the simultaneous presence of unusual linguistic and literary talents in a single person. Translation in the hands of gifted writers is not reproduction but creation, fully deserving of the same informed critical response as other modes of literary endeavor.

NOTES

1. *Faust et le Second Faust de Goethe... traduits par Gérard de Nerval* (Paris: Michel Lévy fréres, 1868), p. 4.
2. Ibid., p. 155, n. 1.
3. Ibid., pp. 39-40. Compare C. F. MacIntyre's version of these lines:

Do as you will. I give you a free hand.
I have no hatred for the like of you.
Among destroyers, you must understand,
the rogue's the least offensive of the lot.
Man's active spirit easily falls asleep;
he's much too readily seduced by sloth.
Therefore, I gladly give him a companion
who prods and twists and must act as a devil.

Goethe, *Faust: Part I* (New York: New Directions, 1949), p. 4. MacIntyre's rendering of the next quotation (p. 40) is: "I am the spirit that always denies! A good thing, too...."
4. Johann Peter Eckermann, *Gespräche mit Goethe* (Wiesbaden: Insel-Verlag, 1959), p. 292.
5. Nerval, *Faust*, pp. 177-78.
6. Nerval, *Œuvres*, Vol. 1 (Paris: Gallimard, 1952), p. 829.
7. Heinrick Heine, "Préface," *Poëmes et légendes* (Paris: Michel Lévy frères, 1859), p. vii.
8. Ibid., p. ix.
9. See W. T. Bandy, "Baudelaire et Edgar Poe," *Revue de littérature comparée*, 41 (1967): 194.
10. Charles Baudelaire, *Correspondance générale*, vol. 4 (Paris: Conard, 1948), p. 277.
11. Cf. Baudelaire, *Critique littéraire et musicale* (Paris: Armand Colin, 1961), pp. 68-69.
12. E. A. Poe, *Aventures d'Arthur Gordon Pym*, ed. Jacques Crépet (Paris: Conard, 1934), p. 251.
13. Léon Lemmonier, "Baudelaire et Mallarmé traducteurs d'Edgar Poe," *Les Langues modernes*, 43 (1949): 48.
14. See W. T. Bandy, "Introduction," Poe, *Seven Tales* (New York: Schocken Books, 1971), p. 8.
15. Cf. Baudelaire, *Correspondance générale, vol. 3, p. 42.*
16. *Critique littéraire et musicale*, pp. 274, 363.
17. *André Gide, Journal 1899-1939*, vol. 1 (Paris: Gallimard, 1965), p. 611.

18. Ibid., p. 735: "This morning I finished translating the first act of *Hamlet*, and I can't push myself further. I've spent three weeks on these few pages at the rate of four to six hours a day. I'm not satisfied with the result. The difficulties are never completely conquered because to write good French one must leave Shakespeare a little too far behind." (editor's translation)

19. Cf. Gide, "Lettre-Préface," *Hamlet* (New York: Pantheon Books, 1945), p. 8.

20. See Elisabeth Brock-Sulzer, "André Gide als Übersetzer Shakespeares," *Shakespeare Jahrbuch*, 92 (1956): 214-15.

21. See Jean-Claude Noël, "L'art de traduction chez Schwob et chez Gide," *Revue de l'Université d'Ottawa*, 39 (1969): 201.

22. Reprinted in Gide, *Préfaces* (Neuchâtel: Ides et calendes, 1948), pp. 45-53.

23. Ibid., pp. 46-47: "A good translator must indeed know the language of the author he's translating, but he must know his own better yet. By that I mean not only must he be capable of writing it correctly but he must know its subtlety and versatility, its hidden resources. This will nearly always mean a professional writer. You don't become a translator by improvisation." (editor's translation)

24. Ibid., p.52: "... It's not only the sense that has to be rendered. It's important to translate sentences, not just words, and to express—without losing anything—thoughts and emotions, as the author would have expressed them if he had written directly in French." (editor's translation)

25. See Jacques Cotnam, "André Gide et le cosmopolitisme littéraire," *Revue d'histoire littéraire de la France*, 70 (1970): 267-85.

Linguistics and Translation

by William H. Snyder

Of those areas of linguistics which have given greatest impetus to the developing science, translation and particularly the problems of machine translation have been most influential and have provided the most significant insights into the nature of language. Since the quest for language universals, the development of transformational and generative grammars, and the reexamination of semantics emerging from this new study of language have brought added dimensions to the understanding of language, one may appropriately ask whether anything of practical value to the translator is to be found here.

The approach to the study of language used by modern linguists is essentially that of the traditional grammarian, i.e., the division of language into grammar (phonology, morphology, and syntax) and lexics (semantics and morphology), the significant difference being the new goal of producing a transformational generative grammar rather than a descriptive grammar. The modern linguist begins, as did the traditional grammarian, with the minimal elements of language, the sounds (phonemes), and proceeds from there to the combination of these into meaningful units, i.e., into words (morphemes/lexemes), and finally to the grouping of words into utterances or sentences. It would be difficult indeed to find a traditional grammar of any language that did not display this tri-partite division into phonology, morphology, and syntax.

The two most important contributions of the recent advances lie in the confirmation of the fact that all language is structured (i.e., rule governed) and in the efforts to produce a grammar that will predict all sentences which can occur in a language (generative grammar) rather than a description of what has already occurred of the traditional grammar. This approach offers a more systematic basis for the descriptions of the structure of language and for the comparison of the grammars of various languages. It follows necessarily from the observations on the universality of the structure of language that if we can devise rules for the structure of a language, then we can also derive rules for the transposition of the structure of one language to that of another; or paraphrasing the frequently cited formula, we may state that to derive the corresponding structure in the language into which we wish to translate, we need to add to the rules of the source language the elements which it does not contain from the target language, and delete from the rules of the source language those elements not contained in the target language. To take a simple example, if we were to translate the English progressive tense into Classic Greek it would lose there its contrast with the other present tense forms of English, while a translation of any past tense form from English would require its relegation to one of the many possibilities in Greek, i.e., imperfect, aorist or perfect tense, thus adding grammatical features and meanings not present in the English. Similiarly, the middle voice of Sanskrit or the present passive participle may be translated systematically into English, but the absence of these features in the target language means firstly, that this feature of Sanskrit will be deleted in the translation; secondly, that the totality of its relationship to the language will be lost as a consequence. Mechanical translation is therefore possible, and in many respects differs little from traditional approaches to translation. The achievements in this direction, moreover, have been truly astonishing, and although the implicit discrepancies remain the same as in the older methods of translation, one must grant that the welcome degree of objectivity sought here is painfully lacking in the more traditional efforts. Consider, by way of example, the translation by H.A. Bellows of the following passage from the "Voluspo" of the Old Icelandic "Edda" (Ed. note: We have regularized the transliterations.):

Voluspo, 49.5

Fiǫlþ veit hon frǒeða, fram sé ec lengra
um ragna rǫc, rǫmm, sigtýva

H.A. Bellows translation:
Much do I know, and more can see
Of the fate of the gods, the mighty in fight.

but more correctly:
much does she know of lore; I see further
beyond the "ragnaroc", the mighty, of the Sigtivar (victory gods).

No mechanical translator would eliminate the change from third to first person, as does Bellows, to bring it into line with his own interpretation of the text, nor would a mechanical translator presume that the quaint English prosody used here could somehow be equated to the starkly vigorous Germanic alliterative verse. Insensitive as it might be to the nuances of language, a machine would still produce a superior translation.

No word in a language stands alone; each one is related to others in a complicated set of grammatical and/or sense relationships which define and delimit its meaning. Those words which have only grammatical function are dealt with under the grammatical analysis, and those which may be characterized as responses in a social context (such expressions as "hello," "good morning," etc.) can be considered to have minimal semantic content. The remaining lexemes, which comprise the overwhelming bulk of the lexemes in the lexicon, characterize the language by the distinctions they impose on the real world; the perception of time, space, color, etc., or of kinship terms, social status, terms for the artisans, etc. These complex relationships vary from language to language to such an extent that there is in fact no one-to-one correlation between words from one language to another, not even between such closely related language groups as German and English or French and Italian. One may discount, of course, the scientific and technical terminology which in itself constitutes a "paralanguage" common to many languages rather than a distinct aspect of one language.

There is no such thing in any language as an utterance without context; every word, every phrase, every attempt at communication must occur in some context—a fact which Freud grasped but unclearly in his observations on errors (slips) in speech, when he proposed that these slips be regarded as expressions of a subconscious level of thought. It is also a basic element which linguists have not yet fully appreciated. A lexeme cannot be translated without regard to its meaning in the particular context; yet in translating, some part of that context is lost in the transition from one set of sense relationships in the source language to a corresponding but not identical set in the target language, a result of the absence of a one-to-one semantic relationship between words of different languages.

The simplest translation would, therefore, be of a text where the "context-suppression" of extraneous sense relationships is greatest. Almost all technical literature from computer repair manuals to cookbooks would fall into this category. A recipe for the preparation of kidney stew, for example, would eliminate all those ties to the functions of bodily organs, animal nature, etc., which James Joyce, by way of contrast, draws on so heavily in *Ulysses*, where he evokes, exaggerates, and distorts through "context loading" these sense relationships, as:

> "He let the bloodsmeared paper fall to her (the cat) and dropped the kidney amid the sizzling butter sauce, and ... he shore away the burnt flesh and flung it to the cat. Then he put a forkfull into his mouth, chewing with discernment the toothsome pliant meat, ..."

The cultural aspects of utterances, when lost or obscured in translation, change and even obliterate the original meaning of a text. In the medieval German epic, *The Nibelungenlied*, the courteous kiss bestowed upon the guest appears as a gesture meant as a genuine display of friendship in:

1665	Diu junge Marcgrâvinne,	kuste die künige alle drî
	(alsam tet ir muoter).	da stuont ouch Hagene bî

> The young marcgravine kissed all the three kings
> her mother did the same, then Hagen was next

but with erotic overtones in the scene where Kriemhilde is permitted to kiss Siegfried (courteously, of course):

297.3	ir wart erloubet küssen	den waetlîchen man.
	im wart in al der werlde	nie sô líebe getân.

> She was permitted to kiss the handsome man.
> Never in all the world did he meet such love.

In both instances the kiss represents a formal, courteous greeting, but the poet plays on the contrast between the empty outward form of the social gesture and the form with real content. The first scene shows the desire to include in the exercise of the formal element a gesture of genuine friendship, which in the second example is extended to a gesture of deep and undying love. In a culture not familiar with this custom, the sharp contrast between the simple form, the form with content, and the form with twofold content, while not entirely lost, is considerably weakened.

In Ari Thorgilsson's *Islendingabók* we read:

Hann sende hingat til lands prest, þann es hét Þangbrandr ok hér kende mǫnnom kristne ok skirþe þá alla, es viþ trú toko. En Hallr á Siþo, Þorsteinssonr, let skirask snimhendes ok Hjalte, Skeggja sonr, ýr Djprsardale ok Gizorr enn huíte, Teits sonr, Ketlsbjarnar sonar frá Mosfelle, ok marger hofþingjar aprer. En þeir voro þo fleire, es í gegen maelto ok neitto. En þá es hann hafþe hér veret einn vetr eþa tvá, þá foŕ hann á braut, ok hafþe veget tva menn eþa þrjá þá es hann hǫfpǫ nitt.

He sent to this country a priest by the name of Thangbrand who taught Christianity to people here, and baptized all those who embraced the faith. Hall Thorsteinsson of Sida let himself be baptized early and so did Hjalti Skeggjason of Thjorsardall and Gizur and the White, son of Teit, son of Ketilbjorn of Mosfell, and many other chieftains: yet those were more numerous who opposed and refused it. And when he had been here a winter or two he went away, having at that time slain here two men or three who had libelled him.

The verb *niþa*, here translated "to libel," seems somehow strange in the context of the English translation. The root of this verb also occurs in the Old Norse words *niþstong* "pole of insult" and *niþareising* "raising a nipstong." This *niþstöng* consisted, according to some accounts, of a horse's head mounted on a pole along with other equally repulsive items for the purpose of working a spell against someone. These are much the same thing as those monstrous figureheads of the Viking warships which were not permitted within sight of the shores of Iceland. The word translated "libel," therefore, probably means something akin to working an evil spell, but, because of our limited knowledge of this custom, the full significance of this passage is lost to us.

These examples are from areas of meaning where the cultural significance is generally accessible or where it is possible to grasp some of the sense of the word from its context even though far removed culturally from our own experience or knowledge. Where there is a lack of information about the culture, as is often the case with older literature, we cannot even begin to grasp the sense relationships which are lost to us simply because of our ignorance of the cultural context. So, for example, in those passages of the *Upanishads* which seem to end with magic formulae, the broader implication of these expressions is simply not clear, as:

Brhadranyaka Upanishad 1 4.5
    so'vet, aham vāva srstir asmi, aham hīdam sarvam
asrksiti: tatah srstir abhavat, srstyam
    hāsyaitasyam bhavati, ya evam veda . . .

He knew, "I indeed am the creation for I produced all this."
Therefore he became the creation. He who knows this
as such comes to be in that creation of his.

Or, turning to the translation of the *Rubaiyat* of Omar Khayyam, it is possible that the attempt at an accurate and conservative translation may be less faithful to the *Sufi* elements of the original than Fitzgerald's rendition, for example:

The Vine had struck a Fibre; which about
If clings my Being - let the Sufi flout;
    Of my Base Metal may be filed a Key,
That shall unlock the Door he howls without.

and if this particular passage indeed contains certain key words of *Sufism* as some claim, then the translation:

When the Original Cause determined by being
I was given the first lesson of love.
It was then that the fragment of my heart was made
The Key to the Treasury of Pearls of mystical meaning.

would be even more appropriate (though poetically less satisfactory).

Finally, the loss both of grammatical elements and meaning in translation may combine to render even the simplest carryover of meaning all but impossible. Consider, for example, the problems of translating the Sanskrit texts mentioned above compounded by complicated plays on words which constitute an integral part of the original text.

> Brhadaranyaka Upanishad 1 4.1
> ... sa yat pūrvo'smat sarvasmāt sarvam pāpmana
> anusat tasmāt purusah; osati ha vai sa tam, yo'smāt pūrvo
> bubhusat; ya evam veda.
>
> Before all this, he burnt evils, therefore he is a person.
> He who knows this, verily, burns up him who wishes to be before him.

with its play in Sanskrit on *purusha*-"man" "earlier" and *us*- "burn," all of which is necessary to grasp the full meaning of the passage.

The limitations of translation which now can be more clearly defined using methods devised by contemporary linguists suggest some possible categories for translation. Obviously, the simplest and most accurate translation will be one involving a minimal number of grammatical features where the context will act to suppress the extraneous sense relationship, ad the goal of the translation is purely informational, such as the technical literature mentioned above. With texts exhibiting more complex grammatical features and more expansive use of semantic content, it becomes necessary to decide whether the ultimate purpose of the translation is to transpose a text from one web of sense relationships to another or to superimpose that web on the target language. The Tieck-Schlegel translations of Shakespeare, for example, created in a sense a "German" Shakespeare, and Martin Luther's translation of the Bible created not only a "German" Bible but produced also new phrases and words which became, as a result of Luther's ability as translator, an integral part of the German language. Not all translations are this fortunate, however. It is said that the German philosopher Arthur Schopenhauer first encountered the *Upanishads* in a poor French translation of an equally inadequate Persian version of the original; despite this twofold injury to the text, Schopenhauer apparently was able to discern the essential meaning of the original. It seems that even in the worst sort of translation of such works as *Oedipus* or *Njals Saga* or of the Bible, some essential part of the original survives, something not considered in our usual linguistic examinations nor contained in the mere story

WILLIAM H. SNYDER

line. Whatever this may be, it is some essential quantity not presently within the scope of linguistic inquiry.

Efforts to convey aspects of a foreign culture in the translation (i.e., to superimpose the sense relationship of the source language on the target language) seem to stand in contradiction to the basic facts of translation, since the attempt to carry the semantic relationships of one language into another is by their nature impossible; the use in the target language of an unfamiliar set of sense relationships tends to create, not an awareness of another cultural environment, but rather to generate a sense of estrangement from the familiar linguistic environment.

In translating texts where little is known of the culture beyond the texts themselves, the most useful approach for those who intend to derive as accurate a picture as possible of that culture from the limited sources available is that used by K.F. Geldner in his translation of the *Rig Veda*. Here the texts are rendered almost word for word and critically annotated. These translations make for dull reading, however, for those whose interests are on a less scientific level. For more generally accessible texts, though perhaps less precise in their scholarly content, some compromise with the various possibilities is necessary, and since readability is, in truth, of major importance in most translations, this aspect becomes crucial although it receives from linguists the least attention.

NOTES

1. Editions used: H.A. Bellows, *The Poetic Edda* (New York: American-Scandinavian Foundation (1923), 1969); Karl Bartsch and Helmut de Boor, eds, *Das Nibelungenlied* (Wiesbaden: F.A. Brockhaus, 1959); Halldor Hermannsson, *Islendingabok* (Ithaca: Cornell University Library, 1930); S. Radhakrishnan, *The Principal Upanishads* (London: Allen and Unwin (1953), 1968); Idries Shas, *The Sufis* (Garden City; Doubleday, 1964).

Translating Arabic Poetry:
An Interpretative,
Intertextual Approach

by Ben Bennani

A translation, whatever the genre may be, is always an interpretation. A translation of a poem, however, does more than interpret; it aims at being a poem itself. Judging by existing translations, I must admit that this seldom happens.

The interpretative process requires systematic analysis of the text, as well as sympathetic understanding of its intertextuality. Here it is understood and accepted that a text has not one but several contexts and that it does not exist in some archival vacuum, but rather stands on broad superstructural premises often referred to as the cultural matrices of the text's language.[1]

In order to give his translation a more seriously intellectual perspective, the translator must, therefore, be willing and able to bridge gaps not only between the source and target languages, but also between the corresponding elements and forces that constitute their respective cultures and societies. In addition to details and principles of composition—style, setting, figures of speech, etc.—the intertextuality of a text should always be of primary concern to the translator. When he ignores it, the process swerves from interpretation and heads into imitation and representation which, by virtue of dwelling on the exteriority of the text, falsifies the text's meaning and violates the humanistic spirit that kindles the artistic fire. When this happens, and it frequently does happen in translating poetry, the translator dons the mask of "the principle of creativity," claiming, but failing to argue validly, that what is basically "untranslatable" must be compensated for with creations emanating from his own single mind.[2]

I do not mean to suggest that changes of any kind (alterations, additions, deletions, etc.) are *not* allowed in literary translation. They are indeed, but only after the translator has penetrated the exteriority of the text, has studied and understood its intertextuality, and has finally had a genuine experience with it comparable to that of the original poet. Furthermore, the importations are acceptable only if the intertextuality of the target text finds them acceptable. Only then do changes cease to be betrayals and become the translator's legitimate and necessary prerogatives, as well as his garnishing parsley. Through interpretative and intertextual lighting, the penumbral effect of a translation which imitation and pure representation too frequently engender totally disappears, and what is so often falsely seen as "untranslatable" poetry soon congeals into *misunderstood* poetry.

Therefore, the translator of poetry must be fluent in and sensitive to the source language; he must know the source language's cultural matrices, its etymologies, syntax, and grammar, as well as its poetic tradition. He must culturally and politically identify himself whole-heartedly with the original poet. He must penetrate the exteriority of the original text and lose himself in its intertextuality. To make the translation become a poem, the translator must also meet successfully the expectations and sensibilities of the poetic tradition of the target language. Thus, the most successful translators of poetry are frequently those who happen to be bilingual and bicultural and, above all, poets in the target language.

To a large extent, the original poem has an immutable text. This can be a great help to the translator. On the other hand, some texts are historically difficult to establish, while many poets often revise their work. Furthermore, successive generations of readers have been known to effect changes in many texts rendering them less than perfectly immutable. The translation (or target poem), one easily guesses, is even less stable. In fact, its integrity as poetry often depends on its ability to change—its malleability at the hands of successive generations of translators. In other words, unless a translation achieves status as canon, it must undergo periodic rebirth.[3]

There are several ways in which translators of poetry solidify their interpretative and intertextual understanding of a given source poem.[4] Some feel that a poem should be translated into prose. Existing prose versions of Homer's *Odyssey* and *The Iliad* and of *Beowulf*, to mention just a few, attest at least to the popularity—if not to the success—of this method. Others insist on verse but fail to agree on a "fixed form." A third group demands verse and insists on none other than the form of the original. A. J. Arberry's translations of the Arabic *Seven Odes*, and Edward FitzGerald's translation of *The Rubaiyyat of Omar al-Khayyam*—follow this approach to translation. A fourth group bridges the first and second contingents in its insistence on both prose and verse. If that is not diverse enough, there is yet another school (more like a recess) whose followers do not rely on the source poem at all; instead, they rely on an intermediary who supplies a literal meaning of the source poem.[5] This method would be not only valid but also indispensible in translating (and transcribing) the oral poetry of the alphabetless languages of North African Berbers and native American Indians and others.

Where form is concerned, my method is a natural or organic one in which content is allowed to determine its own form as the translation develops. Of course, the inseparability of content and form necessitates such a method.

Now that I have introduced my interpretative and intertextual approach to translating poetry, it might be appropriate to introduce Mahmud Darwish, the poet whom I have been translating almost exclusively. I chose to translate Darwish's poetry over a decade ago in the summer of 1967. At first, the compelling force was politics— geopolitics, to be exact. The decision, however,was not made in haste (in the heat of battle as it were). I spent long hours trying to get to know the man and his poetry. Some translators call this developing sympathy, and sympathy is one thing poetry like Darwish's requires much of if it is to be translated successfully. Prior to that commitment, I had fun translating several other poets, mostly Arab and French, but none of them could sustain my interest or win my love and respect the way Darwish had. My translations of some of these poets' works amounted to nothing more than exercises. I suppose the experience itself was beneficial; it taught me that a translator must choose a source text painstakingly and wisely, the way one chooses a very close friend. When I alighted (thanks to the June '67 War) on Darwish's poetry, I knew right away that I had discovered something large and awesome. I also knew that I had to devote many hours of hard work in order to begin to understand the depth and breadth that make up the poet's self and work.

Following the discovery, I had to learn how to read and analyze the poetry in the light of many salient factors, i.e., the intertextual light. The sociocultural problems that confront every serious and sensitive translator were compounded by complex and perplexing political creeds and historical realities. Mahmud Darwish is a Palestinian Arab; he is also a Muslim. On the purely emotional level, my loyalties and prejudices were favorable toward both facts, and, as it turned out, the intertextual light in this case was *not* dim but rather too bright. I was not sure then how to cope with such problems until I discovered the wisdom of balance and moderation.

It happened in the course of research. One day I came across an article written by Darwish in which he pleads with Palestinians in particular and with his wide audience of Arabs in general to dim, in a manner of speaking, the intertextual floodlights which have forced him to be seen largely as a national hero and even a spokesman of a purely political cause, and to see him instead as a poet.[6] All along, however, I was sure of the poetry's strong hold on me. The poetry was unquestionably powerful. Luckily for me, I learned to see him as an artist, yes, but without detaching him from the sober and often painful circumstances of his quotidian life, or from the fact of his involvement with what is essentially a humane cause: the struggle for his and his people's right to life, nationhood, and self-governance. Equally rewarding for me was the fact that from the outset the translations were so well received in the United States, Canada, and Great Britain that I just could not stop.

Other problems were peripheral compared to the above. Nonetheless, they were both challenging and instructive. Darwish's language, for one, is rich and varied, a mixture of classical and modern Arabic on the one hand, and colloquial and spoken Arabic on the other—a mixture of languages in which regionalisms (purely Palestinian words and phrases) are ubiquitous. For example, the Palestinian word for "window" is *shubbak*. It is not even remotely related to its classical and modern equivalent *nafitha*. Neither are *duri* ("swallow," the bird) or *qimbas* (a loose robe or cloak).[7]

Consequently, such language presented, even to the native speaker of Arabic, genuine linguistic challenges. Palestinian Arabic is quite different from the other major Arabic dialects—Moroccan or *maghribi,*

Iraqui, and Egyptian. Therefore, numerous interlanguage insights were gained from translating the Arabic poetry of Mahmud Darwish.

NOTES

1. I am extremely indebted for my intertextual approach to Edward W. Said's *Orientalism* (New York: Pantheon Books, 1978), pp. 12-14.

2. There is no such thing as "untranslatable" material, be it poetry or politics, from the experienced and competent translator's point of view. There is only *misunderstood* material. The single mind sees only the exteriority of a text and tries to imitate. See Said, *Orientalism*.

3. See Marilyn Gaddis Rose's essay "Style in Translation," *Paintbrush* 5, nos. 9 and 10 (1978): pp. 32-36, and André Lefevere's "On Style in Translation," *Paintbrush* 4, nos. 7 and 8 (1977), pp. 7-11.

4. See André Lefevere's *Translating Poetry: Seven Strategies and a Blue Print* (Assen, the Netherlands: Van Gorcum, 1975), and James S. Holmes' "Verse Translation and Verse Form," *The Nature of Translation: Essays on the Theory and Practice of Literary Translation* (The Hague: Mouton, 1970), pp. 91-105.

5. Ezra Pound's translations of Chinese poetry, and more recently his son Omar's translations of Persian and Arabic poems, Robert Lowell's *Imitations*, W. S. Merwin's French and Spanish translations, Robert Bly's Spanish translations, and Daniel Halpern's translations of Mririda n'Ait Attik's songs of the High Atlas are only a few examples of this seemingly popular approach.

6. Mahmud Darwish, "Anquithuna min hatha al-hub alqasi," *al-Jadid*, 14 (March 1969), p. 36.

7. Two works especially helpful to the serious student of Palestinian Arabic are Frank A. Rice and Mayed F. Sa'id, *Eastern Arabic: The Spoken Arabic of Palestine, Syria, and Lebanon* (Beirut: Khayat's, 1960); Elias Nasrallah Haddad, *al-Lugha al-arabiyya al-ammiyya fi filastin* (Jerusalem: s.e., 1946).

Special Considerations
in Drama Translation

by George E. Wellwarth

That dramatic translation is a specialized form of translation with its own rules and requirements seems on the face of it a truism—as indeed it is. It is, however, one of these truisms that are uncomprehendingly accepted whenever they are voiced and then blandly disregarded in practice. Poetic translation encounters no such difficulties or misunderstandings, it being obvious that the translator of poetry must himself have poetic talent. The similarities between the poetic and the dramatic translator are, indeed, striking. The principal requirement for both types of translator is a sense of rhythm. The poetic translator must have a sense of metric rhythm in the target language, as well as the ability to recreate poetic imagery without distortion and without loss of semantic nuance. The dramatic translator, on the other hand, must have a sense of the rhythm of speech patterns, particularly colloquial ones, as well as the ability to recreate the tension of dramatic situations without falsifying the playwright's intention or losing dramatic credibility within the new context.

The dramatic translator faces two principal problems in his work. They are what for want of a better term we must call "speakability" and style. Speakability may be defined as the degree of ease with which the words of the translated text can be enunciated. The writer for the stage, whether he be the playwright or his agent in the new language, must always keep in mind the fact that he is writing a scenario for production. The text of the play is merely a how-to-do-it manual for its animation on the stage. To the playwright this is, of course, obvious: the animation of the descriptive handbook he has written is his whole *raison d'etre*. It should be equally obvious to the translator, but it rarely is. The reason for this is not hard to find. The playwright, if he is any good at all—certainly if he is good enough to be considered worth translating—is by definition a man of the theater. He has usually done everything possible to do in a theater at some time in his career, from selling tickets to sweeping up after the audience has left. The dramatic translator, on the other hand, is primarily a linguist, as indeed he should be, and rarely a theater person at all. While it would be unreasonable to demand that the dramatic translator be as intimately acquainted with theatrical technique as the playwright, for whom it is an absolute necessity, there is no question that some experience as an actor particularly or, failing that, a knowledge of the technique of oral communication, is indispensable. That does not mean that a competent translator without any such experience should avoid the drama, only that the oral/aural aspect of the translation must be kept in mind at all times. There are other ways to achieve this. The mere fact that a translator has no personal experience of oral expression does not necessarily mean that he is incapacitated for dramatic translation, but there are some guidelines that he must follow. In the first place, it is absolutely imperative when translating a play to translate it aloud and to listen carefully to—even to savor—the various versions into which virtually every conceivable line can be translated in English. Having done that, he should, if at all possible, read his translation aloud to someone totally unacquainted with the play, preferably an actor. Actors have the inestimable advantage of being good listeners and having a finely tuned ear for what sounds well on stage and at the same time "lies easily on the tongue." They also tend to come to such a reading without preconceptions about the play, even if it is a well-known one, since they rarely read or permit their minds to become contaminated by any indulgence in critical thought about the little they may have read. What the dramatic translator must watch out for particularly is an excess of sibilants in a sentence, or awkward consonantal clusters that may make a line hard to pronounce rapidly and thus may cause difficulties in sound projection. There should be no great problem in avoiding pronunciation difficulties since English, much more than any other language, offers a rich variety of ways to say anything because of the etymological eclecticism of its vocabulary.

Michael Meyer, the Ibsen biographer and translator, has characterized tautness of expression as the first principle of play translation.[1] Without in any sense discounting the advantages of concision, I would submit that what I have defined as "speakability" is far more important than concision. Of course, concise expressions should be tried for, always, but there is a distinct danger here that the inexperienced translator may end up making a fetish of conciseness and produce a translation that is nothing but a series of hermetically cryptic remarks.

However, important though I think "speakability" is, I do not think that it is the first principle of play translation anymore than I think tautness of dialogue is. The first principle of play translation is style. By style I mean the quality that conceals a translation's provenance. In other words, style is that which causes a play to sound as if it had originally been written in the target language. A play that sounds like a translation is *ipso facto* not well translated. There are, of course, other factors that might make it obvious, or at the very least probable, that the play is a translation, such as setting and costumes, but the language must fall easily and familiarly on the ears of the audience. No audience will give its full attention to a play whose dialogue is stilted, an effect that almost invariably comes from the transposition of the original language's syntax into the target language. The process whereby a play—or any other piece of writing—is transferred from one language to another with the original language's word order and the grammatical constructions peculiar to it carried over into the target language is properly called transliteration. It is not translation. Translation is the *re-creation* of the original language's meaning in the syntax and, in the case of a modern work, in the socially accepted style of the target language. This can only be done by a person steeped in both cultures. Michael Meyer quite correctly states that "another vital principle" of dramatic translation is "that for one person, however bilingual, to do a literal translation and another to turn that into English is no good at all."[2] While this process may be justifiable for obscure languages, where the combination of a person who is bilingual, linguistically sensitive in a literary sense, and equally at home in both cultural ambiences can hardly be expected, it is inexcusable as a device for translating from one of the world's major languages to another. The process of translation and this is as pertinent to nondramatic as to dramatic translation,

> ... will be correct only if the translator has full command over the instrumentalities of both languages and is able to evaluate each word, phrase, [and] construction in respect to their meaning in the total

structure of both languages. Only then will he be able to communicate to people of another culture what the speaker or writer means. The problem of translation brings to the fore the whole complexity of human language; it makes evident the fact that *a single speech performance derives its meaning only in the frame of reference* to the totality of the special language and the corresponding culture. The necessity to trespass into another culture and language in translation *presupposes the capacity of abstraction*. Translation is a representation of things of one world in another world so that they can be grasped in the latter. . . . [We can only translate properly] after we have acquired a real conception of the structure of the new language in relation to the life of the people who speak it. Then the words become representations of the particular approach with which the surrounding world is considered by the people who speak this language, and we begin genuinely to understand the new language. We no longer translate our language to the words of the new language. We think, as one says, in the new language.[3]

The latter part of the quotation refers to translation from the translator's native language to a foreign language, but the basic point remains the same, that the difference between the most rudimentary form of translation, the interlinear transliteration, and the most sophisticated form, the only form acceptable for dramatic translation, is situational conceptualization. In other words, what is required is something more than a morphological transformation of words and a point-by-point transference of semantic values. What is required is the re-creation of a situation or cohesive semantic block in the new language in terms of that language's cultural setting. As Franz Schoenberner put it, a translator's task is essentially a magical one: "A really perfect translator is an alchemist, almost a magician. He must be entirely congenial with the artist whose work he transforms, but he must possess the self-denial not 'to seek his own' but only to reflect the artistic personality of the original author. He has to invent the style in which, let us say, Shakespeare would have written German—and he must not sacrifice the English character of the author and of his work. Translating at its best is, like every kind of art, an act of grace, achieving the seemingly impossible."[4]

Let us see how the seemingly impossible can be achieved. If I am correct in asserting that style is the first principle of play translation, then it is through the achievement of style that the near-magical act of achieving the seemingly impossible must be performed. Style can only be achieved when the translator has a Janus-faced empathy with both of the cultures with which he is working. The anthropologist Bronislaw Malinowski described the nature of that empathy perfectly:

> The translatability of words or texts between two languages is not a matter of mere readjustment of verbal symbols. It must always be based on a unification of cultural context. Even when two cultures have much in common, real understanding and establishment of a community of linguistic implements is always a matter of difficult, laborious and delicate readjustment.
>
> When two cultures differ ... deeply, when beliefs, scientific views, social organization, morality and material outfit are completely different, most of the words of one language cannot be even remotely paralleled in the other.[5]

As far as the nonpoetic drama is concerned, this involves the transference of the colloquial idiom of one language to the colloquial idiom of the other. An example of this that comes up constantly in the translation of modern plays is the curiously emotionless quality of English speech patterns, themselves, of course, a reflection of a culture in which the public expression of emotion is frowned upon. This description of English—and American—behavior patterns as reflected in speech is in no way to be taken in a pejorative sense: the translator's job is not to pass judgment on the culture he is interpreting. In any case, such feelings should not come up since the translator should always be translating *into* his own primary cultural/linguistic milieu. Anyone translating a play from any of the Romance languages or—rather unexpectedly for most people, I think—from German has to wrestle with this problem. The phrases in which emotions, particularly in scenes of love and death, are expressed in these languages seem impossibly, even reprehensibly, florid to the English speaker. They have to be toned down. If not, the translator runs the risk of producing a text that is laughably stilted in English and quite obviously a translation. Sometimes, to be sure, this is unavoidable: the translation of a play about Sicilian peasants would seem even more ridiculous if the characters spoke in the clipped, unemotional mode of English. The only alternatives open to the translator in such a case are a more or less literal version in the hope that the resulting quaintness of the speech patterns gives a flavor of authenticity that overrides the awkwardness, or a transposition of the language into a comparable English language

144

form such as the picturesque and often florid speech pattern of the Irish peasantry. The question here, however, would be whether the translator is justified in adapting as well as translating the play and shifting the locale to another country, for Sicilian peasants discussing the fateful rumblings of Mount Etna and the blighted love of Giuseppe and Santuzza in an Irish brogue would be a bit too much incongruity to take. My own feeling is that the problem has no satisfactory solution and that such plays are best left untranslated. They are usually not any good anyway. However, in the majority of modern plays a normalization of the speech, which in English is largely a matter of toning down, is a necessity. At the same time it must be remembered that there are no rules for dramatic translation. To say that a toning down of the language is a necessity when translating into English is to utter a generalization. A generalization is a statement true at least 51% of the time. Exceptions abound. Toning down is necessary in ordinary dialogue because the everyday speech pattern of English is more subtle and enigmatic than that of most other languages, but there are times when the author has *deliberately* heightened his language in the original; in that case, of course, the translator is obligated to attempt a parallel heightening in the target language. Michael Meyer gives as an example of this, "the final act of *John Gabriel Borkman*, containing the marvellous visionary speeches which Borkman delivers as he looks down from the mountain."[6] Any attempt to tone down such intentionally poetic prose passages results in a translation that sounds like "straw in the mouth."[7] The important thing to remember is that whether one is heightening the language or toning it down, one must always write in such a way as not to grate on the ears of the audience. As George Bernard Shaw aptly observed, "stage usage is one of our few standards of diction"[8]; it behooves the translator to bear in mind that the constantly dynamic speech patterns of his language are extraordinarily sensitive to the influence exercised by the popular literary modes. Thus the translator must have a "two-way ear": he must be permeated with the cadences of his language and at the same time he must be aware of the fact that any neologisms or syntactical innovations that he introduces (assuming that his translation becomes a popular hit) may well creep into the language and become, at least temporarily, standard usage.

The dramatic translator's task is indeed an impossible one. He can

GEORGE E. WELLWARTH

only make an approach, and an altogether tentative approach at that, keeping in mind the principles I have outlined. With constant practice he may move ever close to what Gogol once and for all defined as the ideal translation: one that is like a completely transparent pane of glass through which people can see the original without being aware of anything intervening.[9]

NOTES

1. Michael Meyer, "On Translating Plays," *20th Century Studies (Canterbury),* September, 1974, p. 45.

2. Ibid.

3. Kurt Goldstein, "The Nature of Language," Ruth Nanda Anshen, ed., *Language: An Enquiry into Its Meaning and Function* (Port Washington, N.Y.; Kennikat Press, 1971), pp. 35-36.

4. Franz Schoenberner, *Confessions of a European Intellectual* (New York: Macmillan Co., 1946), p. 178.

5. Quoted in Gene Weltfish, "The Anthropologist and the Fifth Dimension," Stanley Diamond, ed., *Culture in History* (New York: Columbia University Press, 1960), p. 167.

6. Meyer, "On Translating Plays," p. 48.

7. Ibid. The characterization is Sir Laurence Olivier's.

8. G. B. Shaw, *Our Theatre in the Nineties* (London: Constable & Co., 1948,) p. 136.

9. Cited in Meyer, "On Translating Plays," p. 51.

146

Translating for Music:
The German Art Song

by Anne E. Rodda

> A violet in a meadow grew,
> and o'er the vale it fragrance threw,
> so full of life this sweet flow'r!
> There came a gentle shepherdess
> with fairy step and waving tress,
> and trill'd, and trill'd
> like any bird her song. *[1]*

Thus begins a singable translation of Mozart's renowned setting of Goethe's "Das Veilchen." It is obvious that these lines do not quite succeed as poetry in their own right. The translation continues:

> Ah, were I only, thought the flow'r,
> the choicest bloom in nature's bow'r.
> ah! but for one short hour,
> then on that loving maiden's breast
> I soft might lie and sweetly rest,
> and so to her one happy day belong!

> Ah! but alas the maiden fleet,
> with careless mind, beneath her feet
> down trod the tender flow'r!
> It sank, and died, yet glad the while
> it died beneath the maiden's smile,
> and thus, and thus
> receiv'd its wish'd for doom.

> The gentle violet
> was still in death a sweet flow'r!

ANNE E. RODDA

Anyone familiar with the lyric poem "Das Veilchen" will clearly see that these lines fail not only as independent poetry but also as a faithful English rendition of Goethe's poem. It is not necessary to search very far to find reasons for this dual failure. The unnatural juxtaposition of words in phrases such as "it fragrance threw" or "I soft might lie" and the use of quaint expressions such as "with fairy step and waving tress" or "the maiden fleet" or "yet glad the while" combine to create an overall artificial and trite tone. A rigid adherence to the rhyme scheme is partially to blame for the use of such expressions and for the syntactical arrangement that create the artificial ring. As a re-creation of Goethe's poem it falls short chiefly because the translator was making no attempt to achieve a faithful portrayal. Nor was she attempting to write great poetry. The translator was merely writing singable English words (albeit with rhyme) to Mozart's music.

Tradition, rather than the translator, is to blame for the shortcomings of these lines. The translator was following a basically nineteenth-century tradition which dictated that poetry must rhyme and a tradition which focused chief attention on the composer, secondary attention on the sound or meaning of the words, and little or no attention on the original poet or poem. Neither Goethe's name nor the name of any other poet is mentioned anywhere in the collection of forty-three songs in which the cited translation appears, all of which are provided with German, Italian, and English words. Prior to the publication of Jack M. Stein's[2] comprehensive study in 1971 and the text by Elaine Brody and Robert A. Fowkes[3] in the same year, there was virtually no song analysis which did full justice to the poetry of German lieder, and even in the few books which devoted much attention to the poems,[4] first consideration was given to the music. Even now, very few recital programs list the poets' names.

Why was the poetry of German lieder so long neglected by interpreters and abused or slighted by translators? One probable reason for the neglect is the fact that a high percentage of beautiful lieder are set to puerile texts which do not merit interpretation or translation. But the total lieder literature is so vast that even when one has discounted the mediocre texts, there still remain many fine musical settings of great poems. Why is it such a formidable challenge to translate these successfully into a second language?

First, all poetry is difficult to translate, especially good poetry. One must not only capture the theme and the spirit of the original, the ebb and flow of idea and feeling, but one must recreate the rhythm with all its delicate vicissitudes and sound values. The natural rhythm and sound values (i.e., the normal accentuation, the vowel music, the crispness of its consonants) of the second language may well be different from those of the original language. In the words of Brendan Kennelly: "The finding of a right rhythm in translation is like the transplanting of a human heart."[5] Sometimes there are cross-cultural difficulties with the translation as well.[6]

Although the translator dealing with the poem as an independent entity (i.e., without music) faces a difficult task, he is nonetheless usually free to emphasize one of many possible meanings of the printed poem, regardless of what the poet might have meant. He may also be able to catch the ebb and flow and feeling of the rhythm without necessarily using the exact metric scheme of the original poem. The rhythm of poetry is not usually as rigidly prescribed as the rhythm of music, and any line of the poem may contain deviations from the basic metrical pattern.

But the translator of the art song faces a far greater challenge than the translator of the independent poem. In the art song the poem has already been subjected to its first translation, a translation or transposition into the language of music. The conceptual aspects of the poem are now combined with the abstract emotional qualities of the music. While the poem set to music may or may not be a more perfect work of art than the poem alone, it has certainly undergone a substantial metamorphosis. Its sphere is now limited to the composer's interpretation, and its meaning is now more established because of numerous musical elements which influence it.

Jack Stein discusses in considerable detail the musical elements such as rhythm, pitch, duration, appearance of the score, and word-tone painting (*Tonmalerei*) which affect the nature of the poem, which tend to overpower the lyrical values of the poem, and which often cause the music to dominate over it, particularly in the nineteenth-century lied.[7] He illustrates ways in which the rhythm of the music is more aggressive and subjects the poetic meter to the absolute rule of the basic musical beat. He notes that the pitch variations in the melodic line are precisely fixed and tend to suppress the natural intonation and inflectional patterns of the poem, even when they imitate the patterns of the poem. The more delicate and fragile sound values of words in the lyric poem are now merged with the sound values of the music and are likely to be suppressed by it. Stein notes the low tolerance which poetry generally has for extension in time, that the duration of the art song is nearly always longer than that of the recited poem, and that this phenomenon also helps the music to dominate over the poem. The poem set to music has also undergone changes in appearance. Poetry in a musical score communicates quite differently from the printed poem, not only to the ear, but to the eye as well. Quite often it is impossible to reproduce the original poem as it was arranged on paper when attempting to copy it from the vocal score.[8] Finally, any pictorial effects or word-tone painting achieved by the composer's manipulation of rhythm, pitch, duration, appearance, or sound values have a strong impact on the lyric poem and tend to fix the meaning of it. Of the many difficulties facing the translator, such pictorial effects probably pose the greatest challenge of all. Calvin Brown cleverly sums it up:

> The translation of any poem is necessarily a sort of crossword puzzle because of the necessity of attempting to reproduce the form, the meaning, and the feeling of a work which was conceived in a different form. When the poem has been set to music in its original form the difficulty of matching syllables with the music and of making the right words come out on the right notes for the expressive values of the poem is added to the problems of meter, rhyme, sense, and atmosphere, and the problem becomes a sort of three-dimensional cross-word puzzle.[9]

Having established the fact that lieder are generally even more difficult to translate than independent poetry, I wish to discuss various types of musical settings of poetry and to determine what makes certain kinds of settings more problematical than others. Some famous poems have been set to music as many as 171 times.[10] Yet a given translation may be suitable for one setting and not for another setting of the same poem. In the work just quoted Calvin Brown devotes two chapters[11] to defining and illustrating the difference between "literal" settings and "dramatic" settings of lyric poetry. To summarize briefly, he defines a "literal" setting as one which capitalizes on every word that can be imitated in music, and he provides abundant examples from the tenor aria "Every valley shall be exalted . . ." from Handel's *Messiah*.

The phrase, "the crooked straight," for example, could be schematized as follows:

[〜〜〜 _____ .]¹²
The croo- ked   straight

A "dramatic" setting, in Brown's sense of the word, does not exploit every word for which a musical analogy can be found. It considers the total situation, the total context, and attempts to invoke a total mood or to augment the dramatic elements of the whole idea. Schubert's "Erlkönig," a "dramatic" setting of Goethe's poem, is analyzed in minute detail in Brown's book. In this setting the composer creates the illusion of a horse galloping with great urgency through the night without using an exact imitation of the rhythm of a galloping horse. The 145 bars of unbroken eighth-note triplets (albeit in four variations) in the piano accompaniment suggest the idea more effectively than the exact imitation [♩♪ ♫ ♩♪♫/♩]¹³ of the galloping horse on the word *reitet* could have done.¹⁴ Of the two types of settings Brown distinguishes, I believe that "literal" settings of art songs are more difficult to translate than "dramatic" settings. In a literal setting, the translator must match word for word and syllable for syllable in order not to destroy the pictorial effects. This is often impossible, since exact word equivalents in two languages frequently do not have the same syllable count.

Another category of basic types of settings deserves our attention here. There are strophic settings, in which the music used for the first stanza is repeated in all succeeding stanzas, in the manner of a hymn or a folk song. The strophic song does not usually disturb the basic stanzaic arrangement of the original poem. The through-composed *(durchkomponiert)* art song, which uses new music for succeeding stanzas, frequently disturbs or eliminates the original stanzaic arrangement. The strophic and through-composed forms, of course, may be modified and/or combined in a variety of ways, including the cyclical ABA arrangement. The strophic type of setting was the prevalent one for the lieder of the mid- and late eighteenth century, largely because more powerful means of musical expressivity had not yet been developed in the lied and because the keyboard accompaniment had not yet advanced to the point of assuming a solo role. The melody and the harmonic configurations of the accompaniment were still viewed as the unassuming ornamentation to the main component of the song, the lyric poem. Goethe, who believed that a lyric poem should be perfect in itself and should need no further embellishment,[15] naturally preferred the simpler strophic settings and chordal accompaniments of Reichardt and Zelter to the settings of Schubert, which he rejected. In the nineteenth century, many more of the lieder are through-composed and generally more complex in their melodic lines, harmonies, and accompaniments. For the translator, I believe that strophic settings of lieder generally pose fewer problems than through-composed settings. Since the strophic song repeats the same music for all stanzas regardless of their changing content, there is less opportunity for literal imitation of individual words in the melodic line. The translator must naturally make the rhythm match, but he is not in danger of destroying delicate pictorial effects by not being able to match word for word and syllable for syllable. The onus is much more on the singer and the accompanist. The singer must create changes in mood by means of subtle variations in the quality of his singing, by the timbre and color of his sound, through gradations of loudness and softness, through his intrepretation of the fundamental beat, through his sense of line, and by his gestures and facial expressions. The accompanist must deal with the changing content set to the same music through variations in his volume and touch, in partnership with the singer, and in support of the singer telling the story. The brilliant and celebrated accompanist Gerald Moore has provided us with a witty, but serious, recorded lecture-demonstration, "The Unashamed Accompanist."[16] In it he offers a particularly fine example of how the accompanist achieves these variations in a strophic song by Franz Schubert and Wilhelm Müller, "Das Wandern." When the soloist sings that he wishes to wander, to roam, and to be like the happy little millstream rippling on its way to the sea, the accompaniment is flowing, sparkling, and effervescent, light and legato. When the mill wheels are turning and sending the water swirling in a joyful dance, the same accompaniment is light and staccato and imitates the cheerful mood of the personified water. When the heavy millstones turn endlessly, the left hand has a heavy staccato touch, and the right hand plays legato to suggest the endless turning. All these additional artistic aids would tend to help rather than hinder the translator. When dealing with a through-composed song the translator carries a much heavier burden. With new music for new stanzas there is much more opportunity for word-tone painting in the melodic line, and the relationship between word and tone becomes much more critical.

Let us return to our Mozart song to examine the setting in the light of our theoretical discussion and establish the attributes and the pitfalls that it holds for the translator. Although Mozart's "Veilchen" is an eighteenth-century lied, it has nothing in common with the songs of Reichardt and Zelter. It is a through-composed song and in that sense a prototype of the later nineteenth-century lieder, with many of the challenges that they hold for the translator.[17] Mozart's "Veilchen" is also an extremely literal setting of Goethe's poem. Every word which can be pictorialized is exploited, not only in the accompaniment, but also in the melodic line, which is most crucial for the translator. The story it conveys, seriously and delicately told in the poem, is an allegory in which a modest, unassuming flower (a boy; a violet)[18] hopes against hope that the carefree shepherdess whom he loves will honor him when she comes along, by picking him and pressing him to her bosom. If only he were the loveliest flower in creation for only a moment! The careless girl fails to notice him and tramples him. He dies, grateful at least that he has died through her, at her feet.

Every detail of the story is imitated by the music, and hence the words of the translation must match exactly or the total effect is lost. The apoggiaturas and dotted eighth notes in a descending melodic line on the words *gebückt in sich und unbekannt* suggest the hesitating, shy, withdrawn violet with its head bowed. The words in our translation "and o'er the vale it fragrance threw" not only distort the meaning, but destroy the effect completely. A possible alternative might be: "bent down, withdrawn, and known to few," although the phrase has a less poetic ring. Another possibility for *gebückt in sich* might be "and lowly bowed." The main accent in the word must, of course, fall on the downbeat in the music; e.g., *ge-*, the unaccented prefix, falls on the upbeat, and the accented *bückt* falls on the downbeat. One must be careful to retain this principle in the translation. It would be unacceptable, for instance, to use the word "lowly" precisely on the two notes on which *gebückt* appears, for this would cause the syllable "low-" to fall on the upbeat (unstressed) and the suffix "-ly" to fall on the downbeat (stressed). The exact English cognate of *unbekannt*, "unbeknown," would be an ideal translation if it were not somewhat archaic. This phrase is followed by a persuasive diatonic phrase *Es war ein herzigs Veilchen*. The little refrain, rising to a climax on *herzigs*, reinforces the feeling that the violet is charming, sweet, and appealing to the heart; and the climax requires a strong word suggesting this sweetness and appeal. The line "So full of life this sweet flow'r" is not altogether unsuccessful, with the strong word "life" falling on the musical climax. The word "life," however, does not convey the real meaning of *herzig*, and the phrase "so full of life" suggests a vitality and buoyancy that this shy, self-effacing violet, though sweet, lacks. A possible alternative might be "It was a charming violet," but again we face problems. The harsh sound values of the plosive-fricative *ch* [ts] on "charming" are less pleasing to the ear than the softer, gentler aspirated sound of the *h* in *herzig*. The word "lovely," another possibility, is too innocuous as a translation for *herzig*.

In the next phrase, the carefree, indifferent shepherdess comes gamboling along, and her skipping step is imitated both by the staccato eighths in the piano accompaniment and, even more precisely in the melodic line, which exactly imitates a skip [♪♪♪♪].[19] The translation "with fairy step and waving tress" for *mit leichtem Schritt und munterm Sinn* is disastrous, not only because of cross-cultural difficulties that present-day Americans might have with the word "fairy." It fails also because it destroys the pictorial effect of the lightness of step and carefree mood of the original word-tone fusion. Would "so light of step and gay of heart" be better? Would English speakers have cross-cultural difficulties with the word "gay" in its contemporary connotation? Perhaps "with skipping step and cheerful mood" or "with skipping step and merry heart" would succeed. The jubliant end to the first stanza on the words *daher, daher die Wiese her und sang* might be rendered "Along, along the meadow way, and sang." But the words "and trill'd, and trill'd like any bird her song" are not only unfaithful, but ludicrous as well.

The piano interlude which separates stanzas one and two imitates again the girl's carefree frolicking and cheerful singing. As the modest but ever-hopeful violet sees and hears her and senses that his love is doomed to remain unrequited, the music imitates his melancholy as it modulates from G major to the ominous G minor. The first three lines of our cited translation in stanza two are faithful and acceptable, although I would prefer "Oh, just a little while" to "Ah! but for one short hour" as the melodic line longingly rises to the fourth on *Ach! nur* ... The next two lines, however, destroy the delicate word-tone painting of the original. Adversely affected is the word *gepflückt*, which is one of those words whose sounds seem to express the meaning. The word falls at the end of an ascending musical phrase and sounds rather final, like the action of carelessly decapitating a flower. The English word "picked," which creates the same pictorial effect as *gepflückt*, is probably the only acceptable translation for use on the last note of that phrase. "Breast" will not do. "I soft might lie and sweetly rest" hardly matches the amorous tone of *und an dem Busen mattgedrückt*. He really wishes to be smothered on her bosom. The two lines are accompanied by joyous sixteenths in the happy key of B-flat major. The final line of the second stanza, "and so to her one happy day belong," misses the meaning altogether. The modest, almost obsequious, cowering violet entertains no illusions that he can ever permanently belong to his beloved shepherdess. The most he ever hopes for is to be picked and passionately caressed for a short moment, indeed for a brief "quarter hour," *Viertelstündchen*.

As the song moves into the third and final stanza, it modulates back to the dark G minor mode, and the ominous piano chords in G minor portend a cruel end to the dream, described in the recitative that follows. Alas, destiny wills that the maid shall pass by and trample the unnoticed violet. No one could quarrel with "Ah! but alas!" as a translation for *Ach, aber ach*. The devastating and brutal trampling in *ertrat das arme Veilchen* is pictorialized by harsh, unsettling discords, reaching a climax with a piercing diminished seventh chord on *Veilchen*, followed by an even more disquieting pause. "Down trod the tender flow'r" is probably as successful as *ertrat das arme Veilchen*. Here the translator has a rare opportunity to make the translation more effective than the original, simply by finding a one-syllable equivalent of *ertrat* (*zertrat*) such as "smashed" or "crushed" and fixing it precisely on the shattering diminished seventh chord before the pause. *Es sank und starb*, pictorialized by descending seconds, is easily translated: "It sank and died." This is followed by a jubilant return to the joyous key of G major. The broken triads in the accompaniment and the triumphant melodic line, leaping ever higher to *durch sie*, express the violet's victory over self. If he had to die, he was elated that he was privileged to die through her, at her feet. The all-important words, *durch sie*, first expressed in an upward leap of a sixth from A to F-sharp, and a second time in a leap of a fourth from D to high G (the highest note in the piece), are totally lost in the unforgivable translation, "and thus, and thus." Even though the sound values of "her" lack the lustre of the bright *sie*, it would seem that the only acceptable translation of *durch sie* is "through her." The calm little coda, added by Mozart, serves to summarize and to bring the listener back down from an uncomfortable musical height and all too abrupt conclusion. *Es war ein herzigs Veilchen*—It was a charming violet.

Having examined in detail the problems involved in translating German art songs, one is prompted to ask whether German or any other art songs should be translated at all. If so, what is the best way to proceed? What is essential, and what might be sacrificed to achieve the desired effect? Should translations be offered only as an adjunct to the printed recital program, or are there occasions when art songs should be performed in translation?

The answers to these questions are chiefly a matter of personal preference and of accepted concert practice. In many ways it is fortunate that in the concert halls of America audiences expect German lieder to be performed in German. But this should not discourage the serious translator from trying, for he may be able to provide a valuable service to the concert-goer. Translations do not always accompany the printed concert program, and when they are provided they often consist of inadequate and misleading synopses. Translators such as S. S. Prawer, editor-translator of *The Penguin Book of Lieder,*[20] and Philip L. Miller, editor-translator of *The Ring of Words,*[21] have produced indispensable aids to serious students of the art song who are nonspeakers of foreign languages. They have provided excellent and faithful translations of significant numbers of art songs without attempting to make them singable. The translations are printed parallel to the original poems, and they do not consciously attempt to retain rhyme or even a set metrical pattern. They convey the meaning faithfully and naturally, line by line, so that even the monolingual student can frequently ascertain which English word corresponds to which foreign word. For the serious concert-goer, I heartily recommend a practice I use in a course on lieder offered for musicians who are nonspeakers of German. With the Prawer and/or

Miller text in hand, the students listen to recordings of the recited German poetry, and they study the sounds of the German words together with their English meanings. Next they listen to the best musical recordings available, such as those performed by Dietrich Fischer-Dieskau, accompanied by Gerald Moore. We study the literary background of the poems and the relationship of word and tone. Then, with bilingual text and score in hand, we attend our own live performances in the original German or, when fortunate enough, a Judith Raskin master class or a recital by Roberta Peters or Elly Ameling.

With regard to the translator and concert practice, there is always the chance that tradition may change and that the translation may be a brilliant or at least successful rendering of the original.[22] On the matter of how to proceed, I believe that the translator of the art song must begin by understanding the music. Since the musical pattern is fixed, only the words can be manipulated. Carefully planned pictorial effects should be retained wherever possible. It is largely a matter of personal taste, but I believe that if anything can and should be sacrificed to achieve the desired effect, it should be a rigid adherence to a rhyme scheme.

A possible alternative for the translator attempting a singable translation of a German art song might be to avoid attempting to write Goethe or Heine or Eichendorff in English. Let the translator take Goethe's idea, create a new poem in the new language, and attempt to effect a new word-tone synthesis by choosing the English words that come closest to portraying the meaning of the music. Let the translator take full credit and full responsibility with a note—"inspired by Goethe's 'Das Veilchen'."

If tradition should change and audiences should suddenly demand to hear German art songs in English, the translator working for concert performance will have a formidable responsibility. The greater the lyric poem, and the more successful the marriage of word and tone, the more awesome the translator's responsibility will be. Songs such as the Goethe-Schubert "Über allen Gipfeln" or "Gretchen am Spinnrade" or "Erlkönig," the Schumann-Eichendorff "Mondnacht," the Brahms-Platen "Wie rafft'ich mich auf" or Brahms-Heine "Der Tod, das ist die kühle Nacht," and the Goethe-Wolf "Prometheus" represent the highest pinnacle of word-tone achievement. Let the translator who

157

dares to tread there approach such supreme achievements only with reverence.

NOTES

1. Mildred Gauntlett, trans., *Mozart: Songs and Arias*, ed. Josiah Pittman (1816-1886) and Myles Birket Foster (1851-1922), (London: Boosey and Co. Ltd., n.d.), pp. 18-20. A fairly extensive search has failed to uncover the date of this publication. The dates of the editors (taken from the card catalog of Cornell University's Olin Library) would seem to place the publication in the late 1800s or early 1900s. A book entitled *Songs of Scotland*, edited by J. Pittman and published by Boosey and Co., which carries an advertisement for *Mozart's Songs* by Boosey and Co., was purchased for Cornell University in 1905. From this additional information I conjecture that the translation by Mildred Gauntlett was probably published around the turn of the century.

2. *Poem and Music in the German Lied from Gluck to Hugo Wolf* (Cambridge: Harvard University Press, 1971.)

3. *The German Lied and Its Poetry* (New York: New York University Press, 1971).

4. E.g., Richard Capell, *Schubert's Songs* (New York: Macmillan Co., 1957); Eric Sams, *The Songs of Robert Schumann* (New York: W. W. Norton and Co., 1969).

5. "On Translating from Gaelic," *The World of Translation: Papers Delivered at the Conference on Literary Translation* (New York: P.E.N. American Center, 1971), p. 94.

6. This problem is explained and illustrated by several examples, given below.

7. Stein, *Poem and Music in the German Lied*, pp. 10-17.

8. The cited translation of Goethe's "Das Veilchen" was taken directly from the musical score, and the arrangement of the lines in this essay was arrived at by comparison with the original poem.

9. Calvin Brown, *Music and Literature: A Comparison of the Arts* (1948; rpt. Athens, Georgia: Univ. of Georgia Press, 1963), p. 71.

10. E.g., Goethe's "Über allen Gipfeln" or "Wanderers Nachtlied II." This and other statistics are cited in Clarence Eastman's *Goethe's Poems* (New York: Appleton-Century-Crofts, Inc., 1941), p. xxii.

11. Brown, *Music and Literature*, Chapters VI and VII, pp. 53-86.

12. My diagram.

13. My schema.

14. Coincidentally, Brown presents a complete translation, presumably his own, of "Erlkönig," which I find as acceptable as any singable translation I have seen of it; yet he submits it "with some reservations." He advises any reader who can handle the original always "to ignore translations of songs unless the composer actually set the translation rather than the original." *Music and Literature*, p. 71.

15. An interesting article dealing with this question is Jack M. Stein's "Was Goethe Wrong About the Nineteenth Century Lied? An Examination of the Relation of Poem and Music," *PMLA*, 77 (1962), 232-39.

16. Gerald Moore, "The Unashamed Accompanist," Seraphim, Mono 60017. Moore also published an earlier book by the same title.

17. In the sense that it is operatic in its style and derives from the baroque-rococo tradition, it is also atypical of the middle and late eighteenth-century German lied.

18. The text by Brody and Fowkes points out the cross-cultural difficulties which

English speakers might have in accepting a violet as a personified male. The German "Veilchen" is neuter. *The German Lied and Its Poetry*, p. 15.

19. My diagram.

20. (Baltimore: Penguin Books, 1964).

21. (New York: W. W. Norton and Co., 1973).

22. A more faithful and more artistic translation of "Das Veilchen" than the one cited here can be found in Paul Nettl's *Das Veilchen; the History of a Song* (New York: Storm Publishers, 1949). Although it is printed as a poem, together with the original poem, it is coincidentally singable as well. It retains many of the pictorial effects, but it does present certain problems for the contemporary American ear, with the use of words such as "lea" and "unbeknown."

The Economics and Politics of Translation

by Marcia Nita Doron

and Marilyn Gaddis Rose

Item #1. At a large university where a community translation service is integrated with the translator training program, a top administrator's secretary calls the campus catering service to arrange for a reception. After a discussion of the costs entailed by bartending and food preparation, she places an order.

Item #2. Next she calls the translation service because a letter has been received in, say, Russian. The service manager, after securing enough information to make an estimate, tells her the fee. She is horrified; "I'll call the Russian Department," she huffs, "they'll do it for nothing."[1]

Did they? Probably. Probably also with either resentment or ulterior motives, banking for the day when a need to strongarm that particular administrator would arise. The episode, which is assuredly often repeated on college and university campuses, is a paradigm of the problems of the economics and politics of translation, whether the translation is literary or non-literary, scientific, professional, commercial, scholarly, or whatever. Economically, the knowledge, training, and talent for getting material correctly and effectively from one language to another are often considered accidental gifts like good looks and hand-eye coordination, and not properly to be utilized for pay (as beauty and prowess might be). If paid for, translation may be the result of exploitation, intimidation, and marketplace mentality. This, of course, gets us to politics. Translating is often used as a weapon in power struggles. This may be the relatively harmless intimidation by rank as in the examples cited above, but is likely to be more insidious. On a small scale, it may be the exploitation of the translator in a poor bargaining position. On a global scale, translation is an obvious weapon in overt manipulation of readerships and nonliterate audiences. The accidents and decisions of what is allowed to be translated—and, sometimes more important, what is not—see to that.[2] To return to our introductory items, if Academia in the West does not appreciate, let alone rectify, these problems, how can we expect the "real" world to do better?

If for the purposes of discussion, we may separate the American "real" (i.e., nonacademic) world, alternatively beseiging and fortifying the ivory tower, from the rest of the world, the latter may well do better. English-language hegemony, consequent first upon Britannia ruling the waves from, say, 1757 to 1947 (British assumption of *de facto* control of Bengal to Indian Independence) and the briefer American domination from, say, 1945 to 1975 (end of World War II to Southeast Asian setbacks) has meant that Americans have had little need and less motivation to learn foreign languages, while the rest of the world found it highly advantageous to learn English. Further, the fact that France had dominant cultural prestige from 1661 to 1969 (Louis XIV's assumption of personal power to Samuel Beckett's Nobel Prize award) made French an elitist accomplishment, so that Americans with social or intellectual pretensions believed that if they knew French, they would seldom encounter any significant language barriers. (After all, it would be the other person's fault if he didn't know English or French.)

Today, however, the world does not turn to solely English signals (or bow to French etiquette).[3] *Realpolitik* means operational language diversity. This is not the place to deplore wavering foreign-language enrollments in American Academia. Stephen Straight's essay points out that foreign-language mastery is a long-term solution anyway, probably quixotic and certainly inefficient. Equipping the number of Americans who study foreign languages with genuine, if adjunct, translation skills may be more feasible.[4] The recent Library of Congress position paper on translation copyright makes a plea for this strategy.[5]

Yet the situation has not corrected itself in the supply and demand of market needs and translator pool, as happened, for example, with chemists, physicists, and engineers. Why is this? In the United States, surely, we can see the gap as an economic problem. Despite persistent efforts of the American Translators Association, founded in 1959, and the recent complementary efforts of the American Literary Translators, founded in 1978, translators are not generally regarded as members of a profession. Nor is translating generally regarded as a professional activity. (In Academia, we might point out—since many translators are based there—this is as true as anywhere else.) Thus, the response of potential clients is, "if translation is not a professional activity, it need not receive professional remuneration," while potential translators respond, "if translating does not receive professional remuneration, I will train to be something else."

So the demand grows while the supply remains stable. Let's take some examples. As Marcia Doron's "In Scholarly Pursuit" indicates, seminal works in the social sciences are far from being uniformly available in translation. The treasury of landmarks in the history of ideas, broadly defined, is incalculably vast. Until NEH announced its modest translation program in its Research Division in 1977, all such translations ran the risks compounded of chance, political expediency, and the marketplace. Funding was rarely available for translators because it was assumed that scholars doing work in an area would be in command of the requisite languages. Perhaps they would; many disciplines have dominant, if not official languages. Usually scholars cannot command all the languages they need if they wish to be thorough, for even disciplines with language dominance will require learning too many languages for one lifetime. Further, this assumption barred access altogether to general readers and nonspecialists. Commendable as the NEH translation program is, by its own apparent guidelines of attending first to what is in most danger of being lost and second to what has the widest and least ephemeral significance, it eliminates current work and much material written between 1600 and 1975.[6] We might suggest that for current work (e.g., post-Shah magazine fiction, Libyan editorials, etc.) there is often an urgent need. Further, much of the directly relevant background would be found in works written between 1600 and 1975. Much of the treasury of social sciences material, those landmarks in the history of cultures, remains as inaccessible as ever.

In literature, UNESCO has avenues for the translating of masterpieces of member nations (excluding those written in English and French), but these choices must not run counter to the ideology of the sponsoring government.[7] Countering this covert censorship (and minimal funding), the International P.E.N. Club and Amnesty International help beleaguered writers and in so doing often find English readers for underground or anti-Establishment writers. George E. Wellwarth, author of "Some Considerations in Drama Translation," does not mention his own tireless and successful efforts as coeditor of *Modern International Drama*, founded in 1968, to give activist drama a forum. The National Endowment for the Arts has announced a pilot competition for creative writers to translate contemporary materials.

Efforts like his are all the more commendable when we realize that playwrights without a theater or writers in exile, who are usually cut off from the dynamic centers of their own language, may not (and in practice usually do not) write to the taste of American translators trained in Western classics and the relatively neutral traditions of Western criticism. This may be true also of engaged writers and party-line writers.[8] Since translators of literature and scholarship choose works or accept assignments where they feel a real affinity for the author or the material, this means that a restrictive ethnocentrism is operative, or a kind of involuntary censorship of taste. (After all, remuneration being slight at best, translators do not want to translate something positively unpleasant to them.) Even when translators find works appealing, they may back off because the subject matter is too alien for them to feel confident handling it.[9] These factors of taste and expertise further reduce the range and extent of translated material, which is already subject to the random and erratic impulses of the marketplace and the ploys of political expediency.

The result for American readers is that what they find in translation, in both range and extent, whether literary or scholarly, is exotic enough to be piquant, similar enough not to be too unsettling. Desperately as we may need to have an idea of the full gamut of foreign-language expression, there is no way we can expect to be able to form such an idea. Translators are few, their potential task is overwhelming, and their actual task is tokenly appreciated. Thus, we have the paradox that at a time when the economics of capitalistic well-being and the politics of democratic survival could be immensely improved by more widespread translation, anachronistic self-limiting factors continue to prevail within the system. To return once more to our introductory items, the professionals in translation, confronted even in the House of Intellect with less status than the campus caterer, will need to keep their sense of mission (and their sense of humor) for the foreseeable future.

The National Perspective

Recently, I visited Hopewell Village, a restored eighteenth-century iron foundry just outside of Allentown, Pennsylvania. An informative placard in one exhibit noted that despite growing industrialization, the colonies were importing more goods from England and elsewhere than they were exporting. Our current trade deficit is thus a problem which predates the nation.

Recently, there has been a rash of articles in various newspapers and periodicals pointing an accusing finger at our ethnocentric attitude, our physical (and mental?) insularity, our myopic (pompous?) approach to international business. I doubt that a determination could be made as to what percentage of our trade imbalance is directly caused by any of these factors. The fact is, however, that as a nation we are slow to reverse this trend. If anything, an increasing number of monolingual persons are being graduated from our colleges and universities. Congressman Paul Simon points out that only 8% of these institutions require a foreign language for graduation. Further, "In the last three years, 52 American colleges and universities have dropped the teaching of Russian ... (and) 102 have dropped the teaching of German."[10]

Our nation's businesses are constantly bombarded with amusing anecdotes which should illustrate that the need for quality translation exists. The *Wall Street Journal* (5/10/79) ran a front page article which began: "The Marlboro man. Jut-jawed and grizzled, he tirelessly rides the plain, or pauses contemplatively atop his steed to survey the terrain. It sells a lot of cigarettes. In the U.S., that is. In Hong Kong it bombed. It turned out that the Hong Kong Chinese, an increasingly affluent and a totally urban people, didn't see the charm of riding around alone in the hot sun all day." A *New York Times* journalist (5/20/79), in an article entitled "How Malapropisms Abroad Can Hurt," cited the now famous examples of the Chevrolet Nova, which didn't sell in Latin America because Nova bears a striking resemblance to *no va*, meaning "no go;" the General Motors campaign for "Body by Fisher," which translated into "Corpse by Fisher" in many countries;

and the slogan "Come Alive with Pepsi," which in a poor Chinese translation read "Pepsi brings your ancestors back from the grave."

Like the trade deficit, there is nothing new in this currently popular topic of conversation. Well before the President's Commission on Foreign Languages, a staff reporter for the *Wall Street Journal* (1/13/77) cited several tragic examples, such as that of a Mid-East construction worker's death attributed to a "minor" error in the translation of the operating manual for a cement mixer.

Amusing, tragic, costly and/or embarrassing, these anecdotes further reinforce the already established need for professional translations in commercial fields at all levels; this is not limited to multinationals or exporters large and small. With the Census Bureau projecting a 1980 figure of 14 million Hispanic Americans,[11] domestic retailers and service industries can no longer ignore the need for Spanish advertising and for translating warranties, instruction manuals and the like into Spanish.[12]

This lengthy digression serves to introduce the matter at hand which is that despite repeated errors, despite a glaring need, despite the statistics, and contrary to all reason, many firms and government agencies do not hire professional in-house translators, nor do they turn to professional translation services to fill their language needs, if indeed they are aware that they have such needs (one must wonder how much convincing they require). Why? Simply stated, this is where political and economic considerations come into play.

Government agencies and international organizations all too often rely on auxiliary staff members to take on the overflow from their in-house translators. These staff members are often lower-echelon workers who happen to speak a foreign language but lack professional training of any kind. They can be paid substandard fees, the assumption (on my part) being that quality is irrelevant. One government agency unabashedly admitted to paying $2.50 a page for English-into-Spanish translations. Given that a page demands at least two hours of work from rough draft to final typed copy, this is well below minimum wage! It is not the client alone who bears the blame. When investigating the cost of Japanese typesetting, I inadvertently discovered that other agencies were charging anywhere from $20 to $350 for translating 1000 words of English into that language. Since most translators are quick to agree that they are grossly underpaid, one can only guess into whose pockets the bulk of that $350 falls.

Lawyers and consulting firms pass the cost of translation (with a substantial markup) on to their clients, who have little or no recourse when important litigation is at stake, or when their monolingual staff is helpless to dispute the validity or accuracy of the work. The government, however, is indirectly (or directly) charging the taxpayer for its errors. When a Yiddish proofreader found 31 errors on a single page of a seven-page document, the cost of the proofreading alone exceeded that of the translation, not to mention the fact that the type then had to be reset at a considerable expense. The Estonian version of the same document had to be entirely rewritten (and reset).

The federal law which now requires that interpreters be provided for non-English speakers in the courts was passed 14 months ago, but has been implemented in fewer than a handful of states. Even the nation's capital is only now establishing a system for recruiting, testing, screeening and providing court interpreters. A team from California, it is said, will be brought in to set up the system, after a D.C. representative flew there to observe their already operating network. Here, the consideration is surely not economic, for a local solution would obviously be less costly. An outsider can only guess at the political backscratching involved.

The funds which have been allocated for these and other projects never seem to reach the translator, who is exploited from all sides. The client inevitably wants the job completed yesterday and generally fails to recognize the translator's skill with appropriate remuneration. The harried agency executive is caught between the outraged client and the outraged translator, and is hard put to meet the client's demand for a cheaper rate and the translator's plea for better pay. Arbitrating bodies such as the ATA can only throw up their arms in utter desperation and proclaim that everyone is at fault.

The inequities of the "real" world are the same as those of Academia. Perhaps more monies are passed through more hands, but the same ignorance and exploitation prevail.

NOTES

1. The rationale frequently adduced in Academia is that colleagues should help one another. Indeed, collaborators on a specific project, this anthology, for example, may give one another extensive professional help. However, no physicist, for example, would

presume to ask a mathematician who happened to be in command of the requisite language and disciplinary vocabulary to take off three weeks of his life to translate and type a monograph for the sake of collegiality. Yet unless the monograph is translated, it will be closed to the physicist.

2. See my "Avis/Opinion/Warning," *Translation, Agent of Communication*, special issue of *Pacific Quarterly* (Hamilton, New Zealand, January, 1980), ed. by M.G. Rose, p. 4.

3. Ethnic nationalism is usually accompanied by language revival, and we have been in the midst of one of these cyclical recurrences for at least a decade. Wycliffe Bible Translators, Inc., currently identifies 5,103 world languages. See their *The Ethnologue*, Barbara F. Grimes, ed. (Dallas, 1978).

4. Paul Simon, "Progress in the President's Commission on Foreign Languages," *The ATA Chronicle*, 8 (October-November 1979) pp. 16-19.

5. *The Federal Register*, 40 (July 9, 1979) pp. 40147-50.

6. *National Endowment for the Humanities Guidelines*: "pre-modern *original sources* for the history of civilizations ... original sources taken from definitive texts ... sources relevant to early American studies ... translations of scholarly monographs ... translations of literary texts ... major pre-modern classics only ..." Recent awards indicate that "pre-modern classics only" has been replaced by "pre-modern classics chiefly."

7. William Bruce Johnson, "A Publisher's View of Translation," *Translators and Translating* (SUNY Binghamton, 1974) pp. 17-23. It is quite appropriate to query the Educational and Cultural Attache of a foreign country directly for financial aid in publishing a translation.

8. Panels at recent conferences of translators tend to emphasize this inadvertent ethnocentrism. For example, the anti-individualism in current East European literatures may strike a would-be Western translator as faulty characterization; the thematics of Socialist activism may seem like crass propaganda, etc.

9. For example, there are many emerging Francophone literatures which an American translator, comfortable with French life and metropolitan French, finds intimidating because of the implicit cultural matrix; similarly, many works from mainland China rebuff Sino-American translators whose Chinese comes from a different cultural matrix. In this regard, it should be pointed out that lexicographers have not kept pace with language nationalism. This gap seriously restricts the pool of potential translations.

10. Simon, "President's Commission," p. 17.

11. *The Washington Post*, November 20, 1979. *Nation's Business*, December 1979, quotes an independent consulting firm's study which estimates the figure at 20 million.

12. *Wall Street Journal*, October 18, 1979, "Hispanic Market's Sharp Growth is Altering Some U.S. Marketing Tactics."

Contributors

Ben Bennani, instructor of English, Northeastern University (alumnus of SUNY-Binghamton translation program).
>   Editor of *Paintbrush*, translator of *Four Modern Arabic Poets*

Aldo S. Bernardo, professor of Italian and Comparative Literature, SUNY-Binghamton.
>   Senior Dante and Petrarch scholar. Recipient of NEH translation fellowship.

Haskell M. Block, professor of Comparative Literature, SUNY-Binghamton.
>   Authority on Symbolism and Naturalism. Editor and translator of world drama.

Marcia Nita Doron, executive vice-president, Linguatel, Washington, D.C. (alumna of SUNY-Binghamton translation program).
>   Translator from French and Hebrew.

Joseph F. Graham, assistant professor of Comparative Literature, SUNY-Binghamton.

Michael Jasenas, associate professor and curator of Max Reinhardt Archives, SUNY-Binghamton.
>   Director of Comparative Literature M.A. in bibliography. Translator of Hegel.

André Lefevere, professor and chairman of Germanic Studies, University of Antwerp, visiting professor of Comparative Literature, SUNY-Binghamton.
>   Author of *Translating Poetry; Literary Translation: the German Tradition*; co-author of *Littérature comparée: traduction littéraire* and *Uitnodiging tot de Vertaalwetenschap*.

Zoja Pavlovskis, associate professor of Classics and Comparative Literature, SUNY-Binghamton.
>   Editor and translator of *Apollonius of Tyre*.

Anne E. Rodda, associate professor of German, Ithaca College.
>   Editor and translator of anthology of short stories by modern German women writers. Lieder specialist.

Marilyn Gaddis Rose, professor of Comparative Literature, director and founder of Translation Research and Instruction Program, SUNY-Binghamton.

Translator of French Decadent literature.

Stephen David Ross, professor and chairman of Philosophy, SUNY-Binghamton.

Authority on metaphysics, aesthetics, and philosophy of language.

William H. Snyder, professor of Linguistics and German, SUNY-Binghamton.

Specialist in historical linguistics, foreign-language pedagogy, English as Second Language.

Sandro Sticca, professor of French and Comparative Literature, chairman of Romance Languages, SUNY-Binghamton.

Medieval studies scholar and editor.

H. Stephen Straight, associate professor and chairman of Linguistics, SUNY-Binghamton.

Specialist in Yucatec (Mexico) and child language. Fulbright scholar in Romania, 1979-80.

Immanuel Wallerstein, distinguished professor and chairman of Sociology, SUNY-Binghamton.

Director of Fernand Braudel Center, editor of Braudel *Review*. Translator of Ladurie and Braudel.

George E. Wellwarth, professor of Theater and Comparative Literature, SUNY-Binghamton.

Co-editor of *Modern International Drama*. Editor and translator of contemporary Catalan, French, German, and Spanish drama.

Index

170

Index